WHY CATHOLIC?
JOURNEY THROUGH THE CATECHISM

THE
PROFESSION
OF FAITH

What We Believe

The publisher gratefully acknowledges use of the following:

The Scripture quotations contained herein are from the New Revised Standard Version Bible (containing the Old and New Testaments with the Apocryphal/Deuterocanonical Books), copyright © 1989 by the Division of Christian Education of the National Council of the Churches of Christ in the U.S.A., and are used by permission. All rights reserved.

English translation of the *Catechism of the Catholic Church* for the United States of America copyright © 1994, United States Conference of Catholic Bishops—Libreria Editrice Vaticana. English translation of the *Catechism of the Catholic Church: Modifications from the Editio Typica* copyright © 1997, United States Conference of Catholic Bishops—Libreria Editrice Vaticana. Used with permission.

Copyright permission for posting of the contents and index of the *Catechism of the Catholic Church* on the RENEW International Website was granted by "Administrazione del Patrimonio della Sede Apostolica," case number 344.333 on May 14, 2001, Vatican City.

For online access to an interactive site allowing users to search the full text of the *Catechism of the Catholic Church*, go to www.vatican.va/archive/ENG0015/_INDEX.HTM

Excerpts from the English translation of *Lectionary for Mass* © 1969, 1981, International Committee on English in the Liturgy, Inc. All rights reserved.

NIHIL OBSTAT
Reverend Lawrence E. Frizzell, D.Phil.
Archdiocese of Newark Theological Commission
Censor Librorum

IMPRIMATUR
Most Reverend John J. Myers, J.C.D., D.D.
Archbishop of Newark

Cover design by James F. Brisson

Library of Congress Control Number: 2005900776

ISBN 1-930978-35-9
(Previous edition ISBN 1-930978-14-6)

RENEW International
1232 George Street
Plainfield, NJ 07062-1717
Phone   908-769-5400
Fax   908-769-5660
www.renewintl.org
www.WhyCatholic.org

Printed and bound in the United States of America.

Contents

✝ ✝ ✝

Acknowledgments

✝ ✝ ✝

RENEW International gratefully acknowledges those who have contributed to this work:

Artists and their Publishers

Ansgar Holmberg, CSJ for the illustrations on pages 4, 16, 20, 28, 32, 33, 38, 39, 45, 51, 58, 64, 70.
Copyright © Living the Good News. Used by permission of the publisher.

Gerardine Mueller, OP for the illustrations on pages 9, 15, 22, 37, 44, 53, 56, 63, 71. Used by permission of the artist.

Joan Smith, OP. for thehe illustrations on pages 2, 8, 26. Used by permission of the artist.

Therese Denham, CSJ for the illustration on page 47. Used by permission of the artist.

Suzanne Phillips, SND for the illustration on page 57, which is taken from *Witness to the Gospel* artwork. Used with permission. Copyright © NCCV, Chicago, IL.
For Catholic Church vocation resources contact NCCV 773.955.5453/www.nccv-vocations.org.

Piloters

Small Christian community members who piloted the materials and offered helpful insights.

Foreword

✝ ✝ ✝

My calling as a bishop challenges me to ever seek means to assist solid faith formation and growth in holiness. Foundational in meeting this need is the *Catechism of the Catholic Church,* which so magnificently conveys the wisdom of the Holy Spirit in guiding the Church's tradition in following Jesus Christ.

The Introduction to the U.S. bishops' document *Our Hearts Were Burning Within Us* speaks of how disciples of Jesus share in proclaiming the Good News to the entire world.

> Every disciple of the Lord Jesus shares in this mission. To do their part, adult Catholics must be mature in faith and well equipped to share the Gospel, promoting it in every family circle, in every church gathering, in every place of work, and in every public forum. They must be women and men of prayer whose faith is alive and vital, grounded in a deep commitment to the person and message of Jesus.

Why Catholic? Journey through the Catechism is well designed to enable this goal to become reality. It faithfully breaks open the contents of the *Catechism* for reflection and assimilation by individuals or participants in small faith-sharing groups. The sharing enables participants to take greater personal ownership of their faith and to move from an inherited faith to deep faith conviction.

This exploration of divinely revealed truth has a formative effect on peoples' lives. The "yes" of consent to faith emulates Mary's fiat, her "yes" to God's will. A prayerful openness to God's will is the path to holiness.

Why Catholic? seeks to be an instrument for faith formation and a call to holiness. Saints in everyday life are the strength of the Church, which is always renewing itself in fidelity to the mission of Christ and in service to the needs of our society. I heartily commend this effort in making the *Catechism of the Catholic Church* more accessible to the faithful.

Most Reverend John J. Myers, J.C.D., D.D.
Archbishop of Newark

Introduction

✝ ✝ ✝

Many Catholics have inherited the faith without knowing why they are Catholic. They have never been exposed to the solid faith formation provided by the *Catechism of the Catholic Church*. For that reason, RENEW International has taken the four parts of the *Catechism* and has developed this series, *Why Catholic? Journey through the Catechism*.

Why Catholic? is an easy-to-use tool for individuals and/or small faith-sharing communities to reference, read, pray over, and treasure the rich resources of the *Catechism of the Catholic Church*. By using these materials, we hope participants will study the *Catechism of the Catholic Church* in greater depth, internalize its teachings, share faith in Jesus Christ, learn more about their faith, and let their faith illuminate every aspect of their lives.

The reflections offer people a "taste" of the content of the *Catechism*. *Why Catholic?* is not intended to be a compendium or a total summary of the *Catechism*, but rather, a way for people to try to become more faithful to the teachings of the Church. We encourage people to read sections of the *Catechism* before, during, and after each session.

In a way, *Why Catholic?* is a guidebook to the *Catechism*. Yet it is much more. It invites readers and participants to a mature faith by nourishing and strengthening laywomen and men in their calling and identity as people of faith.

These four books may be a way for people to uncover their own story, their own journey about being Catholic. What does it mean to be Catholic? Why do Catholics remain Catholic? Why did they become Catholic? To assist in discovering their story, we recommend participants keep a journal and after each session spend some time journaling key beliefs of the Catholic Church and their personal insights. What a valuable treasure they will have to meditate on and perhaps share with others.

Part One of the *Catechism of the Catholic Church* focuses on the great mysteries of our faith. In Part Two the emphasis is on celebrating our faith in sacramental liturgy. Part Three helps to explain the moral teachings of the Catholic faith. Part Four looks more deeply at our relationship with God and how we nurture that relationship in prayer.

This first book from the *Why Catholic?* Series, *The Profession of Faith: What We Believe*, looks at the truths that we, as Catholics, believe and explores these basic tenets of our faith. It offers insights on what it means to be Catholic, following "the oldest Roman catechism," the Apostles' Creed.

If you are gathering in a small community, you may wish to meet either in two six-week blocks of time or over twelve consecutive weeks to cover all the sessions. Your community may also wish to use the other three books based on the *Catechism*:

The Celebration of the Christian Mystery: Sacraments (Part Two),

Life in Christ: Walking with God (Part Three), and

Christian Prayer: Deepening My Experience of God (Part Four).

May these reflections lead you to a closer, more vibrant relationship with our loving God.

N.B. Throughout the *Why Catholic?* Series constant and direct reference is made to the *Catechism*. Many sentences in the **Exploring the Catechism** sections are direct quotes. To make these easily identifiable, direct quotes are in bold print. Elsewhere, what the *Catechism* says is summarized and paraphrased: this is in regular print. Whether directly quoted or paraphrased, material from the *Catechism* is identified by the paragraph number from the *Catechism* in bold print and in parentheses, that is, **(000).**

Faith-Sharing Principles and Guidelines

When we gather as Christians to share our faith and grow together in community, it is important that we adhere to certain principles. The following Theological Principles and Small Community Guidelines will keep your community focused and help you to grow in faith, hope, and love.

Principles

- God leads each person on his or her spiritual journey. This happens in the context of the Christian community.
- Christ, the Word made flesh, is the root of Christian faith. It is because of Christ, and in and through him, that we come together to share our faith.
- Faith sharing refers to the shared reflections on the action of God in one's life experience as related to Scripture and the faith of the Church. Faith sharing is not discussion, problem solving, or Scripture study. The purpose is an encounter between a person in the concrete circumstances of his or her life and a loving God, leading to a conversion of heart.
- The entire faith-sharing process is an expression of prayerful reflection.

Guidelines

- Constant attention to respect, honesty, and openness for each person will assist the community's growth.
- Each person shares on the level where he or she feels comfortable.
- Silence is a vital part of the total process. Participants are given time to reflect before any sharing begins, and a period of comfortable silence might occur between individual sharings.
- Persons are encouraged to wait to share a second time until others who wish to do so have contributed.
- The entire community is responsible for participating and faith sharing.
- Confidentiality is essential, allowing each person to share honestly.
- Action flowing out of the small community meetings is essential for the growth of individuals and the community.

A Note to Small Community Leaders

Small Community Leaders are ...

- People who encourage participation and the sharing of our Christian faith.
- People who encourage the spiritual growth of the community and of its individual members through communal prayer, a prayerful atmosphere at meetings, and daily prayer and reflection on the Scriptures.
- People who move the community to action to be carried out between meetings. They are not satisfied with a self-centered comfort level in the community but are always urging that the faith of the community be brought to impact on their daily lives and the world around them.
- Community builders who create a climate of hospitality and trust among all participants.

Small Community Leaders are not ...

- **Theologians:** The nature of the meeting is faith sharing. Should a theological or scriptural question arise, the leader should turn to the pastor or staff to seek guidance.
- **Counselors:** The small communities are not intended for problem solving. This is an inappropriate setting to deal with emotionally laden issues of a personal nature. The leader is clearly not to enter the realm of treating people with emotional, in-depth feelings such as depression, anxiety, or intense anger. When someone moves in this direction, beyond faith sharing, the leader should bring the community back to faith sharing. With the help of the pastor or staff, the person should be advised to seek the assistance of professional counseling.
- **Teachers:** The leaders are not teachers. Their role is to guide the process of the faith sharing as outlined in the materials.

N.B. The *Why Catholic? Small Community Leader Guide* is designed to assist small community leaders in their crucial role of facilitating a *Why Catholic?* small community.

How to Use This Book

Whenever two or more of us gather in the name of Jesus, we are promised that Christ is in our midst (see Matthew 18:20). This book helps communities to reflect on the Scriptures and the *Catechism of the Catholic Church*. It is most helpful if some members of the group or the group as a whole have the Scriptures and the *Catechism* at their meeting.

Those who have met in small communities will be familiar with the process. In this book based on the *Catechism*, however, there is particular emphasis on the great mysteries of our faith. These reflections make demands upon our reflective nature and help in the formation of our Catholic values. THEREFORE, IT IS IMPORTANT THAT PARTICIPANTS CAREFULLY PREPARE FOR THE SESSION BEFORE COMING TO THE MEETING. They are encouraged to read and reflect on the session itself, the Scripture passage(s) cited, and the sections of the *Catechism* referenced.

If the community has not met before or if participants do not know each other, take time for introductions and to get acquainted. People share most easily when they feel comfortable and accepted in a community.

Prayer must always be at the heart of our Christian gatherings. Following any necessary **Introductions**, sessions begin with a time of prayer—**Lifting Our Hearts.** There are suggested songs, some of which may be found in the parish worship aid. Other appropriate songs may be used. The Music Resources section (page 74) indicates where the suggested songs may be found as CDs or cassettes, in printed form, or in some cases, as downloadable mp3 files. If songs are copyright, remember you need to request permission before making copies of either the words or the music. The contact information for permissions can be found in the Music Resources section.

Each week, an action response—**Living the Good News**—is recommended. After the first week, the leader encourages participants to share how they put their faith in action by following through on their **Living the Good News** commitment from the previous session.

Following **Lifting Our Hearts,** and **Living the Good News,** there is an initial reflection on the *Catechism* entitled **Exploring the *Catechism*.** The next section, **Pondering the Word,** offers a Scripture reference that one participant proclaims aloud from the Bible. Together, the *Catechism* and Scripture selections will give the community members the opportunity to reflect on what Jesus has said and to share their faith on the particular topic. Sharing could take about 15 minutes.

Next, the small community continues **Exploring the *Catechism*** and then considers the **Sharing Our Faith** questions. Faith-sharing groups vary greatly in their background and composition. In some sessions, the group may wish to start with the question: What insights into my faith did I gain from this session? Explain. Allow approximately 25 minutes for **Sharing Our Faith,** making sure the last question is always considered.

In coming to closure, each session offers some ideas for an individual or group action—**Living the Good News.** Here, participants reflect on how God is inviting them to act during the coming week—how to bring their faith into their daily lives. The ideas presented are merely suggestions. It is important that group members choose an action that is both measurable and realistic.

Each session then concludes with **Lifting Our Hearts.**

Suggested Format of the Sharing Sessions (1½ hours)

Introductions (when the group is new or when someone joins the group)	
Lifting Our Hearts	10 minutes
Sharing the Good News	5 minutes
Exploring the *Catechism*	10 minutes
Scripture: Pondering the Word and Sharing Question	15 minutes
Exploring the *Catechism* (continued)	10 minutes
Sharing Our Faith	25 minutes
Living the Good News	10 minutes
Lifting Our Hearts	5 minutes

Sharing beyond the Group

As a group, you will be using this book as the focus for your sharing. You should consider how the fruits of your sharing can be taken beyond the confines of this group. For example, if you are parents, you could be asking what part of your faith exploration can be shared with your children. RENEW International has designed a resource, entitled RENEWING FAMILY FAITH, to help you achieve exactly this.

RENEWING FAMILY FAITH offers a two-page full-color bulletin for every Session contained in the *Why Catholic?* faith-sharing books. You will find a full description of this invaluable resource on pages 76-77.

Session 1
Desire for God

†††

Suggested environment

Bible, candle, and, if possible, the *Catechism of the Catholic Church*
Begin with a quiet, reflective atmosphere.

Lifting Our Hearts

Song

"Jesus, Come to Us," David Haas (Oregon Catholic Press-OCP)

Poem

(read by one member of the group)

> I fled Him, down the nights and down the days;
>   I fled Him, down the arches of the years;
> I fled Him, down the labyrinthine ways
>   Of my own mind; and in the midst of tears
> I hid from Him, and under running laughter.
>   Up vistaed hopes I sped;
>   And shot, precipitated,
> Adown Titanic glooms of chasmèd fears,
>   From those strong Feet that followed, followed after.
>   But with unhurrying chase,
>   And unperturbèd pace,
> Deliberate speed, majestic instancy,
>   They beat—and a Voice beat
>   More instant than the Feet— …
> "Naught shelters thee, who wilt not shelter Me."

From "The Hound of Heaven" (lines 1-14, 51)
by Francis Thompson (1859-1907)

Prayer

(prayed alternately by two people or two groups)

Side 1   I cry to you, my God.
        Listen to me.

Side 2   I have tried to do your will.
        I have acted in love.
        I have never raised my hand in violence.
        I have always tried to walk in the paths you set before me.

Side 1   Sometimes I get weary, Lord—weary trying to find you.
        Yet I know you are there.
        You will never forget me.

Side 2   Grant me, Father, the grace of persevering love
        and the experience of your presence.
        Help me recognize it is you who calls me,
        who beckons me.
        Reveal yourself in some special way today that I may find
        true rest.

Exploring the *Catechism*

As human beings, we often ask questions such as: Where do I come from? Where am I going? What kind of meaning does my life have? Who is God? How does he work in my life and in our world?

As Catholics, we believe that **[t]he desire for God is written in the human heart** because God creates us and constantly draws us to deeper communion **(27).** There is within each person an internal desire for God, a deep yearning for the holy.

Reflect together on these words of Jesus.

Scripture: Pondering the Word   Luke 12:32-34

Sharing Question

- Jesus said, "For where your treasure is, there your heart will be also." In what ways have I experienced my faith in God as a treasure?

Exploring the *Catechism* (continued)

We are religious beings who have in so many ways throughout the centuries **given expression to** [our] **quest for God in … religious beliefs and behavior: in … prayers, sacrifices, rituals, meditations, and so forth (28)**.

But sometimes this "intimate and vital bond … to God" (*Gaudium et spes* 19 § 1) **can be forgotten, overlooked or … rejected** by people **(29)**. Yet no matter how much we forget or reject him, God never ceases to seek us out to show us the true ways to happiness **(30)**.

Our search for God requires **every effort of intellect, a sound will, "an upright heart," as well as the witness of others who teach** [us] **to seek God.** What a striking paradox: God has created us with an intense desire for himself and yet we must be willing to respond with all our being. St. Augustine, who looked in so many places to try to have his desires filled, finally found God and reminds us in his prayer: "You have made us for yourself, and our heart is restless until it rests in you" (*Confessions* 1, 1, 1) **(30)**.

How can we come to know God? Our *Catechism* describes the **proofs for the existence of God, not in the sense of proofs in the natural sciences, but rather in the sense of "converging and convincing arguments," which allow us to attain certainty about the truth (31)**. We can look to the physical world—the message of creation, and the human person, the voice of conscience—and **arrive at certainty about the existence of God … (46)**.

We certainly know that there is orderly direction in our world. Our first astronauts, upon looking at the earth, reminded all of us of the power of God and his creation. Today we hear an increasing number of scientists who, through their work in physics, microbiology, astronomy, etc., conclude that there must be a Creator of this magnificence.

Physicists tell us that it is becoming apparent that each particle in the universe has a way of "knowing" every other particle. Rather than science simply explaining away the creation of the world in solely scientific terms, we see more and more scientists recognizing that faith is not dead, but very much alive. As more scientific discoveries are made, scientists are seeing —through the eyes of faith—the great miracle that God has created.

[T]he world's order and beauty can give us the **knowledge of God as the origin and the end of the universe (32).**

Secondly, we recognize that the human person has a soul, with an openness to truth and beauty, a sense of moral goodness, freedom, and the voice of a conscience, **with ... longings for the infinite and for happiness. ...The soul, the "seed of eternity we bear in ourselves" ... can have its origin only in God (33). ...** [We] **come to know that there exists a reality which is the first cause and final end of all things, a reality "that everyone calls 'God'"** (St. Thomas Aquinas, *Summa Theologica* I, 2, 3) **(34).**

We know the existence of God, but how can we speak about him? It is difficult at times because **our knowledge of God is limited** and so is our language **(40). Our human words always fall short of the mystery of God (42).** Thomas Aquinas reminds us that we may not be able to grasp totally who God is, but we can know who he is not and we can listen to how others stand in relation to him **(43).** Therefore, it is important for us to share our experience of God with one another. While he is a mystery, we can grasp glimpses together as a community of believers.

As Catholics, we all are united in one common faith. We believe in God. Any other differences we have are minor compared to this great truth. Whether we are male or female, dark-skinned or light-skinned, conservative or liberal, Democrat, Republican, or Independent, what matters most is our relationship with God and his creation.

Sharing Our Faith

- How do we see "proof" for the existence of God in our physical world?
- When did turning to God give me peace?
- What are the things I have sought to fill my spiritual hungers? How have I responded to God's grace?

- How will I care for my spiritual life in a special way this coming week? How will I put my life into God's hands?

Living the Good News

Determine a specific action (individual or group) that flows from your sharing. This should be your primary consideration.

When choosing an individual action, determine what you will do and share it with the group. When choosing a group action, determine who will take responsibility for different aspects of the action.

The following are secondary suggestions:

- Keep a journal, and each day write the ways you yearn for God.
- Reflect on the excerpt from Francis Thompson's poem "The Hound of Heaven." Journal your feelings about the poem or discuss it with another member from your group.
- Write down the ways you see the power of God at work in our world today. Share them next week with your group.
- Share your belief in the existence of a loving God with a co-worker, neighbor, or relative.

As my response to the gospel of Jesus, this week I commit to _____

_____ .

Lifting Our Hearts

Pray together

> O God, our Father,
> in response to your grace,
> we are constantly searching for you.
> Sometimes it is difficult to sustain this search.
> Help us this day to listen
> to the sound of your unhurrying feet,
> as you reveal yourself to us
> and seek us out in the crossroads of our conversations,
> our busy actions,
> and the empty silences of our lives.
> Help us to be at rest in you.

We ask this through your Son, Jesus Christ our Lord
in the unity of the Holy Spirit. Amen.

To conclude, offer each other a sign of God's peace.

Looking Ahead

- Prepare for your next session by prayerfully reading and studying **Session 2, God's Revelation: Tradition and Scripture** and paragraphs 50-141 of the *Catechism*.
- Remember to use *RENEWING FAMILY FAITH* (see pages 76-77) and its helpful suggestions on how to extend the fruits of your sharing beyond your group, especially to your families.

Session 2

God's Revelation: Tradition and Scripture

✝✝✝

Suggested environment

Bible, candle, and, if possible, the *Catechism of the Catholic Church*
Begin with a quiet, reflective atmosphere.

Lifting Our Hearts

Song

"We Walk by Faith," verses 1-2, Marty Haugen (GIA)

Pray together

Gracious God and Father,
open our hearts and minds
to understand your words.
Let your grace fall upon our hearts and bear fruit.
Give us the courage to hear and reflect
on all that you have taught.
Help us to lay aside our former way of life and old selves
and acquire a fresh, spiritual way of thinking.
Remind us that we can be "new persons"
created in your image.
And remind us that we must hear and believe your Word
in order to be those persons.
We ask these things through Jesus Christ our Lord. Amen.

Sharing Our Good News

*Share how you did with your **Living the Good News** from the previous session.*

Exploring the *Catechism*

God loves us so much that he created us with the ability to know his will and love him **beyond** [our] **natural capacity (52).** Throughout history,

God has always communicated gradually to us through various stages of revelation **(54-64)**. Finally, God fully revealed this **plan of loving goodness** by sending us Jesus **(50)**.

The teachings of Jesus were given to his followers and were handed on to us from his disciples and apostles. These teachings and traditions developed in the Church through the power of the Holy Spirit. This body of truth grew and became known as Sacred Tradition and Sacred Scripture. Tradition continues to grow today through the teaching and preaching of the pope and bishops who, being faithful to their call, have received it through apostolic succession. It is also enhanced through the contemplation and study of all the people of God **(80-82)**.

Both Sacred Scripture and Tradition arise from the same divine source, the mystery of God's love for us in Jesus Christ and the power of the Holy Spirit. The Church honors both as united in revealing the mystery of Jesus Christ. Both pass on the apostolic heritage and remain normative for the Church in every age **(80-82)**.

The early Christian community was very aware that Jesus was the full revelation of God and kept the stories of Jesus alive. St. Peter exhorts the early Christians to be attentive to Christ and his message.

Scripture: Pondering the Word   2 Thessalonians 2:13-17

Sharing Question

- Paul is very clear that we need to give equal importance to Scripture (what is handed on by letter) and to Tradition (what is handed on by word of mouth). How have the Scriptures and/or Tradition revealed God's message to me?

Exploring the *Catechism* (continued)

Jesus instructed **"the apostles to preach the Gospel, which had been promised beforehand by the prophets, and which he fulfilled in his own person. … In preaching the Gospel, they were to communicate the gifts of God to all …" (75)**. In keeping with the Lord's command, the Gospel was handed on in two ways:

— *orally* … **"by the spoken word …, by the example they gave, by the institutions they established, what they … received … from … Christ, from his way of life …, or … at the prompting of the Holy Spirit"**; *(Dei Verbum 7)* [and]

— *in writing* **"by those … who, under the inspiration of the same Holy Spirit, committed the message of salvation to writing"** *(Dei Verbum 7)* **(76)**.

In order to assure that the integrity of the gospel and the teachings of Jesus would be preserved, **"the apostles left bishops as their successors. They gave them 'their own position of teaching authority'"** *(Dei Verbum 7 § 2; St. Irenæus, Adversus hæreses 3, 3, 1: PG 7, 848; Harvey, 2, 9)*. … **This living transmission, accomplished in the Holy Spirit, is called Tradition … (77-78)**. The task of giving an authentic interpretation of the Word of God has been entrusted to the living, teaching office of the Church—the pope and the bishops in communion with him **(100)**.

In practice, the popes and bishops do not make decisions on matters of faith and morals in total isolation. They reflect with "the body" of faithful Catholics who have particular gifts **(91)**. Good dialogue between theologians and the teaching office of the Church has been mutually beneficial in building up the Body of Christ. Good dialogue is necessary among all the faithful. The pope and the bishops, who receive the power and inspiration of the Holy Spirit by reason of their office, are the ones who are responsible for authentically handing on the truths that have been revealed to us **(100)**.

God is the author of Sacred Scripture (105). As Catholics, we understand that the Scriptures (which are made up of 46 books in the Old Testament and 27 in the New Testament) are the inspired Word of God. God chose certain people, who, using their own knowledge, vocabulary, and literary skills, were inspired by the Holy Spirit to teach the truths that he wanted taught **(105-108)**.

When the evangelists wrote the gospels, they did not write in isolation but used accounts that had been told many times. They were testimonies to the faith of the early Christian communities. They conveyed the events of Jesus' life and his teachings as understood by the community under the guidance of the Holy Spirit. It was, in fact, a series of local councils of early Christian believers in North Africa (held at Hippo in AD 393 and at Carthage in AD 397 and 419), that determined the Canon of Scripture (the list of biblical books recognized as divinely inspired). The gospels truly have a social and communal dimension.

The books of the Bible were written in different literary forms. **In Sacred Scripture, God speaks to man in a human way. To interpret Scripture correctly, the reader must be attentive to what the human authors truly wanted to affirm and to what God wanted to reveal to us by their words** (cf. *Dei Verbum* 12 §1) **(109). In order to discover** *the sacred authors' intention*, **the reader must take into account the conditions of their time and culture, the literary genres in use at that time, and the modes of feeling, speaking, and narrating then current (110).**

The Second Vatican Council indicates three criteria for interpreting Scripture .... 1. *Be especially attentive "to the content and unity of the whole Scripture." ...* 2. *Read the Scripture within "the living Tradition of the whole Church." ...* 3. *Be attentive to the analogy of faith* **(111-114).** The "analogy of faith" refers to the fundamental coherence and connectedness that informs the truth of Revelation. In addition, we need to read Scripture while distinguishing between the literal sense and the spiritual sense **(115-119).**

It is important for us to understand the style of writing as well as the times in which the Scriptures were written. It is equally important to see the New Testament as a reflection of the early Christian community moving with the guidance of the Holy Spirit. It would be misleading to have people make their own individual interpretations of the Bible since they would thus be separating themselves from the community of believers and the body of truth from which the Scriptures originated. Christ spoke with authority and the Church presents the Scriptures to us under the authority of the Holy Spirit.

Sacred Scripture permeates and nourishes all aspects of the life of the Church. We are encouraged to learn and "know" the Scriptures in order to know Jesus **(131-133).**

Sharing Our Faith

- Share a favorite Scripture passage. How has this passage affected the way I live my life?
- The Scriptures include narratives about and letters to the early Christian community and how God worked in the lives of people and their circumstances. What does that mean for me today in how I understand the Scriptures?
- Why is it so important in our Church that Tradition be guided by the Holy Spirit? What would happen if each person interpreted the Scriptures individually?
- What can I do to get to know the Scriptures more fully? What will I do?

Living the Good News

Determine a specific action (individual or group) that flows from your sharing. This should be your primary consideration.

When choosing an individual action, determine what you will do and share it with the group. When choosing a group action, determine who will take responsibility for different aspects of the action.

The following are secondary suggestions:

- Study paragraphs 50-141 of the *Catechism*. Journal your feelings about them.
- Attend a Scripture study class to learn more about the Scriptures.
- Read a passage from the Bible every day. Focus on one phrase or sentence from that passage and repeat it often during the day.
- Read stories from the Bible to your children, grandchildren, or other youngsters. Perhaps use a children's Bible, depending on the age of the children.

As my response to the gospel of Jesus, this week I commit to _____

_____ .

Lifting Our Hearts

Response: Spirit of God, Spirit of Goodness, fill us.

That we may acquire a desire to learn Scripture
and an appreciation of the Sacred Tradition handed on to us in the
Church, we pray:

That we may be enlightened by the study of Sacred Scripture,
we pray:

That the love of Sacred Scripture will always fill our hearts,
we pray:

That we may understand and respect the value of Church Tradition,
we pray:

Spontaneous petitions …

Response: Spirit of God, Spirit of Goodness, fill us.

Pray together

God, our Heavenly Father,
you have revealed yourself in many ways.
You have given us Sacred Tradition and Sacred Scripture
to teach us more about you.
Direct our hearts and minds
to read and ponder your words
and love them with all our hearts.
Give us this grace, O God.
We ask this in the name of Jesus. Amen.

Looking Ahead

- Prepare for your next session by prayerfully reading and studying
  Session 3, Faith: I Believe, We Believe and paragraphs 142-231 of
  the *Catechism*.

- Remember to use *RENEWING FAMILY FAITH* (see pages 76-77) and its
  helpful suggestions on how to extend the fruits of your sharing
  beyond your group, especially to your families.

Session 3

Faith: I Believe, We Believe

✝✝✝

Suggested environment

Bible, candle, and, if possible, the *Catechism of the Catholic Church*
Begin with a quiet, reflective atmosphere.

Lifting Our Hearts

Song

"We Walk by Faith," verses 3-4, Marty Haugen (GIA)

Psalm 111 *(prayed alternately by two people or two groups)*

Side 1   Praise the LORD!
          I will give thanks to the LORD with my whole heart,
              in the company of the upright, in the congregation.

Side 2   Great are the works of the LORD,
              studied by all who delight in them.

Side 1   Full of honor and majesty is his work,
              and his righteousness endures forever.

Side 2   He has gained renown by his wonderful deeds;
              the LORD is gracious and merciful.

Side 1   He provides food for those who fear him;
              he is ever mindful of his covenant.

Side 2   He has shown his people the power of his works,
              in giving them the heritage of the nations.

Side 1   The works of his hands are faithful and just;
              all his precepts are trustworthy.

Side 2	They are established forever and ever, to be performed with faithfulness and uprightness.

Side 1	He sent redemption to his people; he has commanded his covenant forever. Holy and awesome is his name.

Side 2	The fear of the LORD is the beginning of wisdom; all those who practice it have a good understanding. His praise endures forever.

Sharing Our Good News

*Share how you did with your **Living the Good News** from the previous session.*

Exploring the *Catechism*

There is probably no issue more critical for us today than faith. We live in a time of escalating change and confusion. The underlying question for us is: Do we believe?

God constantly invites us into a grace-filled life of love and goodness. We have a choice. By faith, we can respond to him, "Yes, my Lord, I offer myself to you. Do with me as you wish." Sacred Scripture calls this response "the obedience of faith" **(142-143).**

Listen to the Letter to the Hebrews, which talks about the faith of biblical figures and the call to faith that each of us has been given.

Scripture: Pondering the Word   Hebrews 11:1-12

Sharing Question

- How does my faith compare with the faith of those in this reading from Hebrews, or with the faith of Mary and those in New Testament accounts, like Peter, Elizabeth, or Mary Magdalene?

Exploring the *Catechism* (continued)

It is the Holy Spirit who enables us to believe. What is it that we believe?

We believe in God the Father and we believe we can trust him absolutely. We believe in Jesus who was sent by his Father to reveal the mystery of the Trinity to us. We believe in the Holy Spirit who reveals to us who Jesus is. "… **No one comprehends the thoughts of God, except the Spirit of God**" (1 Corinthians 2:10-11). **Only God knows God completely: we believe *in* the Holy Spirit because he is God (150-152).**

Faith is a free gift from God and allows us to glimpse eternal life when we will see God "face to face" (1 Corinthians 13:12) **(162-163).** Without God's grace, it is impossible to believe in the Trinity or to live good moral lives. **Believing is possible only by grace and the interior helps of the Holy Spirit.** We assent to divine truths by both our human intellect and the grace of God **(154-155).** Therefore, while faith is a gift, it also requires our response, our "yes." **What moves us to believe is not** our mere human reason, but our acceptance of the power and authority of God and the movement of his Spirit within us **(156).**

Faith is *certain*. It is more certain than all human knowledge because it is founded on the very word of God who cannot lie (157). "Faith *seeks understanding*" (St. Anselm) …. Faith opens the eyes of our hearts **to a lively understanding of the contents of Revelation: that is, of the totality of God's plan and the mysteries of faith … (158).** Faith and science do not contradict one another. **[M]ethodical research in all branches of knowledge, provided it is carried out in a truly scientific manner and does not override moral laws, can never conflict with the faith, because the things of the world and the things of faith derive from the same God** (*Gaudium et spes*, 36 §1) **(159).** What a wonderful world God created! Through our faith, we can know his wonders most deeply.

Because faith is a gift, it is not merited but is freely given and must be freely received. Jesus **invited people to faith and conversion, but never coerced them (160).** Faith can in fact be lost, and in order to preserve it **we**

must nourish it with the word of God; we must beg the Lord to increase our faith; we must help our faith grow through acts of charity and we must root our faith in the Church (cf. Mark 9:24; Luke 17:5; 22:32) **(162). The world we live in often seems very far from the one promised us by faith. Our experiences of evil and suffering, injustice, and death, seem to contradict the Good News; they can shake our faith and become a temptation against it (164). It is then we must turn to the** *witnesses of faith*: people like Abraham and the Virgin Mary **(165).** It is then that we must witness to one another the faith that each of us has been given.

Faith is a personal act … [b]ut faith is not an isolated act. … Our love for Jesus and for our neighbor impels us to speak to others about our faith. Each believer is thus a link in the great chain of believers. I cannot believe without being carried by the faith of others, and by my faith I help support others in the faith (166). In the Apostles' Creed each of us proclaims, "I believe" and in the Nicene Creed, as a community we proclaim, "We believe." As believers—both individually and communally—we proclaim we will live in God's way; we will live a life of faith.

Sharing Our Faith

- Was there a point in my life in which the faith that I inherited truly became *my* faith? Explain.
- How did God lead me to choose faith? Share specific factors that led you to respond to God and become a believer.
- How does my faith help me to live a graced moral life? How does living a good moral life help me grow in faith?
- What do I need to have my faith grow stronger?

Living the Good News

Determine a specific action (individual or group) that flows from your sharing. This should be your primary consideration.

When choosing an individual action, determine what you will do and share it with the group. When choosing a group action, determine who will take responsibility for different aspects of the action.

The following are secondary suggestions:

- Read and reflect on the Apostles' Creed or the Nicene Creed during this coming week. Stop after each section and consciously proclaim your belief aloud.
- Write in a personal journal about your faith.
- Share your beliefs with a friend or someone from your parish.

As my response to the gospel of Jesus, this week I commit to _____

_____ .

Lifting Our Hearts

Pray the Apostles' Creed together. Stop after each sentence for quiet reflection.

I believe in God, the Father almighty,
    creator of heaven and earth.

I believe in Jesus Christ, his only Son, our Lord.
    He was conceived by the power of the Holy Spirit
        and born of the Virgin Mary.
    He suffered under Pontius Pilate,
        was crucified, died, and was buried.
    He descended to the dead.
    On the third day he rose again.
    He ascended into heaven
        and is seated at the right hand of the Father.
    He will come again to judge the living and the dead.

I believe in the Holy Spirit,
    the holy catholic Church,
    the communion of saints,
    the forgiveness of sins,

the resurrection of the body,
and the life everlasting. Amen.

The Apostles' Creed
English translation
by the International Consultation on English Texts

Each person turns to the one next to him or her and traces the sign of the cross on that person's forehead while saying:

"In the name of the Father,
and of the Son,
and of the Holy Spirit. Amen."

Looking Ahead

- Prepare for your next session by prayerfully reading and studying **Session 4, The Trinity** and paragraphs 232-278 of the *Catechism*.
- Remember to use *RENEWING FAMILY FAITH* (see pages 76-77) and its helpful suggestions on how to extend the fruits of your sharing beyond your group, especially to your families.

Session 4
The Trinity

✝✝✝

Suggested environment

Bible, candle, and, if possible, the *Catechism of the Catholic Church*
Begin with a quiet, reflective atmosphere.

Lifting Our Hearts

Song

"Praise God, from Whom All Blessings Flow" (public domain)

Psalm 67 *(prayed alternately by two people or two groups)*

Side 1   May God be gracious to us and bless us
         and make his face to shine upon us,

Side 2   that your way may be known upon earth,
         your saving power among all nations.

Side 1   Let the peoples praise you, O God;
         let all the peoples praise you.

Side 2   Let the nations be glad and sing for joy,
         for you judge the peoples with equity
         and guide the nations upon earth.

Side 1   Let the peoples praise you, O God;
         let all the peoples praise you.

Side 2   The earth has yielded its increase;
         God, our God has blessed us.

Side 1   May God continue to bless us;
         let all the ends of the earth revere him.

Sing together once again

"Praise God, from Whom All Blessings Flow."

Sharing Our Good News

*Share how you did with your **Living the Good News** from the previous session.*

Exploring the *Catechism*

As Christians, we make a profound act of faith every time we say, "In the name of the Father, and of the Son, and of the Holy Spirit." We proclaim that we believe in one God who is Father, Son, and Spirit: the Holy Trinity.

The mystery of the Most Holy Trinity is the central mystery of Christian faith. ... It is the mystery of God ... (234).

It is the mystery of love—a dynamic eternal love—the three persons of the Trinity fulfilling God's **"plan of his loving goodness" of creation, redemption, and sanctification (235).**

Scripture: Pondering the Word   John 14:9-21, 25-26

Sharing Question

- Jesus, as we see in John's Gospel, reveals his intimate relationship with the Father and the Holy Spirit and invites us to participate in this Trinitarian communion. How "at home"are the Father, Son, and Spirit in my life?

Exploring the *Catechism* (continued)

The Trinity is a mystery of faith in the strict sense, one of the "mysteries that are hidden in God ..." (*Dei Filius* 4) **a mystery that is inaccessible to reason alone or even to Israel's faith before the Incarnation of God's Son and the sending of the Holy Spirit (237).**

When the Father sent Jesus, God was revealed as Father, Son, and Spirit. Jesus revealed this dynamic unity of loving communion and called all his followers to participate in this love relationship.

We call God **"Father" inasmuch as he is Creator of the world** (cf. Deuteronomy 32:6; Malachy 2:10) **(238).** He is the Father from whom the Son proceeded from all eternity. **He is neither man nor woman: he is God (239).**

Jesus called God his Father and tells us he was sent by his Father to be our Savior. Jesus himself revealed that the Father is in relation with the Son. They are in total and loving relationship with each other. They are one. "No one knows the Son except the Father, and no one knows the Father except the Son and any one to whom the Son chooses to reveal him" (Matthew 11:27) **(240).**

Before his Passover, Jesus announced the sending of "another Paraclete" (Advocate), the Holy Spirit. ... The Holy Spirit is thus revealed as another divine person with Jesus and the Father (243). The Spirit is sent to the apostles and to the Church ... after Jesus' glorification and completes the **fullness** [of] **the mystery of the Holy Trinity (244).** The Holy Spirit is the Spirit of both the Father and the Son **(245).**

From the beginning, the revealed truth of the Holy Trinity has been at the very root of the Church's living faith ... (249). During the first centuries, through various councils, the Church sought to clarify the notion of the Trinity in order to deepen its own understanding of the mystery. The Church concluded:

1. *The Trinity is One.* **We do not confess three Gods, but one God in three persons.**

2. *The divine persons are really distinct from one another.* In other words, God as Father, Son, and Holy Spirit **are not simply names designating modalities,** but distinct persons.

3. *The divine persons* **live in relationship with** *one another.* They have one nature. **"Because of that unity the Father is wholly in the Son and wholly in the Holy Spirit; the Son is wholly in the Father and wholly in the Holy Spirit; the Holy Spirit is wholly in the Father and wholly in the Son"** (Council of Florence [1442]) **(253-255).**

A magnificent part of the mystery of the Trinity is not only that God is a dynamic communion of love, but also that we are called to participate in that communion of love. By our Baptism, we are "born again" into the divine life. By the indwelling of the Holy Spirit in our hearts, we are enabled to share intimately in the life of the three Divine Persons. We are caught up into the "love life" of God. In John 14, Jesus tells us that he is in the Father and the Father is in him, and that we in turn are invited into that loving dynamic. Here is our mandate as Christians: we are invited to be a community of love.

Eternal Truth! Eternal Fire! Eternal Wisdom!

Grant us Your gentle & eternal blessing. ✝

SAINT CATHERINE of SIENA

Community is possible for us—not because of any merits of our own, but because God is community and he invites us to participate in his Divine Life. Those who obey the commandments of God will be loved by him in that beautiful bond that the Father has with his Son, Jesus (John 14:21). When God helps us to live a life of unselfish love, we are, in fact, living the "life" of the Holy Trinity. **The ultimate end of the whole divine economy is the entry of God's creatures into the perfect unity of the Blessed Trinity. ... [W]e are called to be a dwelling for the Most Holy Trinity ... (260).**

Sharing Our Faith

- Share your understanding of the mystery of the Trinity. How do I relate to God the Father, to Jesus the Son, or to the Holy Spirit?

- Jesus says, "Those who love me will keep my word, and my Father will love them, and we will come to them and make our home with them" (cf. John 14:23). Share experiences you have had of a loving dynamic community. How have I been aware that I was participating in the mystery of the Trinity?

- What are some ways in which I am invited into the communion of love (in my family, parish, community, etc.)?

- How do I strive to invite others into a communion of love?

Living the Good News

Determine a specific action (individual or group) that flows from your sharing. This should be your primary consideration.

When choosing an individual action, determine what you will do and share it with the group. When choosing a group action, determine who will take responsibility for different aspects of the action.

The following are secondary suggestions:

- Read and reflect on paragraphs 232-278 of the *Catechism*.
- Each time you make the Sign of the Cross, be aware of the loving relationship between God the Father, God the Son, and God the Holy Spirit.
- If you are a godparent, speak with or write to your godchild about the love that God has for each of us.
- In your prayer journal, list the people who have welcomed you into the community of love and describe how that friendship/relationship brought you to a closer understanding of the Trinity. Write a letter to the persons(s) describing how they touched your life.

As my response to the gospel of Jesus, this week I commit to _____

_____ .

Lifting Our Hearts

Close with spontaneous prayers of adoration.
In conclusion, pray together

O my God,
Trinity whom I adore,
help me forget myself entirely
[and to rest] in you,
unmovable and peaceful
as if my soul were already in eternity.
May nothing be able to trouble my peace
or make me leave you,
O my unchanging God,
but may each minute bring me more deeply
into your mystery!

Grant my soul peace.
Make it your heaven,
your beloved dwelling and the place of your rest.
May I never abandon you there,
but may I be there, whole and entire,
completely vigilant in my faith,
entirely adoring,
and wholly given over to your creative action.

From "Prayer to the Trinity"
by Blessed Elizabeth of the Trinity (1880-1906)

Looking Ahead

- Prepare for your next session by prayerfully reading and studying **Session 5, The Mystery of Creation** and paragraphs 279-421 of the *Catechism*.
- Remember to use RENEWING FAMILY FAITH (see pages 76-77) and its helpful suggestions on how to extend the fruits of your sharing beyond your group, especially to your families.

Session 5

The Mystery of Creation

†††

Suggested environment

Bible, candle, and if possible, the *Catechism of the Catholic Church*
Begin with a quiet, reflective atmosphere.

Lifting Our Hearts

Song

"Canticle of the Sun," Marty Haugen (GIA)

Pray together

May you be praised, O Lord, in all your creatures,
especially brother sun, by whom you give us light for the day;
he is beautiful, radiating great splendor,
and offering us a symbol of you, the Most High. …

May you be praised, my Lord, for sister water,
who is very useful and humble, precious and chaste. …

May you be praised, my Lord, for sister earth, our mother,
who bears and feeds us,
and produces the variety of fruits and dappled flowers and grasses. …

Praise and bless my Lord, give thanks and serve him in all humility.

From the *Canticle of the Creatures*
by St. Francis of Assisi (1182-1226)

Sharing Our Good News

*Share how you did with your **Living the Good News** from the previous session.*

Exploring the *Catechism*

We have often heard the Old Testament account of the story of creation.
"In the beginning God created the heavens and the earth" (Genesis 1:1).

The New Testament reveals that God created everything by the eternal Word, his beloved Son. The Church's faith likewise confesses the creative action of the Holy Spirit, the "giver of life," "the Creator Spirit" ... (cf. the Nicene Creed; hymn *Veni, Creator Spiritus*) **(291). Creation is the common work of the Holy Trinity (292).**

Scripture: Pondering the Word   Genesis 1:1—2:4a

Sharing Question

- We believe that God created the world with great wisdom, love, and good order. Throughout the creation process, "God saw that it was good" (Genesis 1, verses 4, 10, 12, 18, 21, 25, 31). Through creation, we share in God's goodness. How do we experience God's goodness in creation?

Exploring the *Catechism* (continued)

God did not create the world as a finished product with complete perfection, but rather he created the universe **"in a state of journeying"** (*in statu viae*) **toward an ultimate perfection yet to be attained ... (302).** He

continues to guide our "journeying" through "divine providence." **God cares for all, from the least things to the great events of the world and its history (303). Jesus asks for childlike abandonment to the providence of our heavenly Father ...:** "Therefore do not be anxious, saying, 'What shall we eat?' or 'What shall we drink?' ... Your heavenly Father knows that you need them all. But seek first his kingdom and righteousness, and all these things shall be yours as well" (Matthew 6:31-33; cf. 10:29-31) **(305).**

One of the Lord's marvelous gifts to human beings is the ability to cooperate freely with his plans. God created us **to be intelligent and free ... in order to complete the work of creation ... (306-307).**

God freely loves us and asks us to realize we can do nothing without him. We are not God, but we are like God in that we are in relationship with him and thus carry out his providential plan for all of creation.

Many of us ask the questions: If God is so good and loving, how can he permit evil to exist? Why is there suffering in this world? Would a loving God allow war and violence, illness and death, hate and destruction?

There are no easy answers. In many ways, the existence of evil and suffering is mysterious. **Only Christian faith as a whole constitutes the answer to this question: the goodness of creation, the drama of sin, and the patient love of God** who meets us by covenants, by sending Jesus, by empowering us with the Holy Spirit, by gathering us as his Church, by giving us sacraments, by giving us a blessed life **(309).**

Perhaps the cross best gives insight into the mystery of suffering. The Father's only Son, Jesus, suffered and died to redeem us **(571).** Jesus gave meaning to suffering and death and taught us that through it we would receive new life. Many times those who have suffered greatly look to the cross as their means for comfort and deeper understanding. Often in suffering, people come to know God in a deeper way and trust him more fully. Often in suffering, people recognize their total dependence on God and fall in love more deeply with him. Those who suffer may even help others through their suffering. *There is not a single aspect of the Christian message that is not in part an answer to the question of evil* **(309).**

God created us out of love and because of that great love gave us the gift of freedom. Yet, he permits evil because he respects the freedom of creation. Love requires freedom. No one can love and not give the beloved freedom. Because we have been given a free will, we, as human beings, can cause evil. We can go astray. We can do evil things. Yet, in the midst of evil, God is so powerful as to bring good out of evil. Out of the terrible evil of persecution, suffering, and death, God brought about the greatest of goods, our salvation **(312).** That does not mean evil is good but rather "… that in everything God works for good for those who love him" (Romans 8:28) **(313).** We believe **that God is master of the world and of its history,** but God's ways **are often unknown to us**. Only when we see God "face to face" (1 Corinthians 13:12) will we be able to understand fully the ways of God **(314).**

God created the universe with wonderful order. Each creature was given *its own particular goodness and perfection ….* **Man must therefore respect the particular goodness of every creature, to avoid any disordered use of things which would be in contempt of the Creator and**

ALL YOUR WORKS SHALL GIVE THANKS TO YOU, O GOD.

PSALM 145.10

would bring disastrous consequences for human beings and their environment (339). We are all interdependent.

The order and harmony of the created world results from the diversity of beings and from the relationships which exist among them (341).

As human beings, we were created with a wonderful nature. We read in Genesis that we were created "in the image of God, male and female, we were created" (cf. Genesis 1:27). God created man and woman **to be a communion of persons,** to be in partnership with one another **(372).** We were given both a body and a soul. Our souls are our innermost selves, the *spiritual principle* in us **(363).** Our souls are **created immediately by God** and so do not perish when separated from the body at death but are **reunited with the body at the final Resurrection (366).**

Sharing Our Faith

- What experience have I had in which God brought good out of a painful or evil situation?
- How have I been able to help others through a painful experience I have had? How did I invite God to be part of that experience and any healing that followed?
- In what personal experience was it difficult for me to love someone and allow him or her freedom? In what way did God's grace empower me?
- What do I consider a respectful attitude and manner in relating to people? What can I do to address the problems of sexism and racism? How can I help the world see the dignity of all people as children of the same loving Father?

Living the Good News

Determine a specific action (individual or group) that flows from your sharing. This should be your primary consideration.

When choosing an individual action, determine what you will do and share it with the group. When choosing a group action, determine who will take responsibility for different aspects of the action.

The following are secondary suggestions:

- Observe the beauty of creation. Take a walk in the woods. Admire the beauty, reflecting on and thanking God as you walk.
- Visit someone who is in a nursing care facility.
- Invite someone who is looking for comfort or healing to take a walk with you.
- As a sign of your respect for creation, plant some flowers or trees around your neighborhood or invite some people to clean a section of a park.

As my response to the gospel of Jesus, this week I commit to _____

_____ .

Lifting Our Hearts

Thank you, God, for the gifts you have given us
by your creative power …
earth and water, air, plants and animals,
other people, and our own individual lives.

We live, dear Creator,
longing to be aware of the beauty and gifts of life,
yearning to appreciate and receive these gifts of love from you,
and desiring to delight in, reverence,
and share what we have come to know as expressions of your love.
We ask for eyes to see, ears to hear, and hearts to love.

O Mysterious One, we also struggle to see your face.
In the midst of darkness, evil and suffering
—that is personal, communal, and global—
we yearn for reassurance that you are near and that you know all.

Help us to remember
that you are light in the darkness,
peace in the pain,
faithful in tragedy and hardship,

and promise to bring all
—somehow and at some time—
to good.

Ever-loving God,
we are in awe of your power and majesty,
your beauty and grace,
and most of all your unending love.
May the gifts you have so generously offered
be received and shared through Jesus, the Christ. Amen.

If possible, as a group go outside and offer prayers of thanksgiving for our beautiful universe.

Looking Ahead

- Prepare for your next session by prayerfully reading and studying **Session 6, The Incarnation** and paragraphs 422-511 of the *Catechism*.
- Remember to use RENEWING FAMILY FAITH (see pages 76-77) and its helpful suggestions on how to extend the fruits of your sharing beyond your group, especially to your families.

Session 6

The Incarnation

†††

Suggested environment

Bible, candle, and, if possible, the *Catechism of the Catholic Church*
Begin with a quiet, reflective atmosphere.

Lifting Our Hearts

Song (Even if it is not the Christmas Season, because of the topic, a Christmas carol is sung.)

"Angels We Have Heard on High" (public domain)

Pray slowly together the "Gloria" from Mass.

Glory to God in the highest,
      and peace to his people on earth.

Lord God, heavenly King,
almighty God and Father,
      we worship you, we give you thanks,
      we praise you for your glory.

Lord Jesus Christ, only Son of the Father,
Lord God, Lamb of God,
you take away the sin of the world:
      have mercy on us;
you are seated at the right hand of the Father:
      receive our prayer.

For you alone are the Holy One,
you alone are the Lord,
you alone are the most High,
      Jesus Christ,
      with the Holy Spirit,
      in the glory of God the Father. Amen.

Sharing Our Good News

*Share how you did with your **Living the Good News** from the previous session.*

Exploring the *Catechism*

Jesus means in Hebrew: "God saves." The angel Gabriel announced that good news before Jesus was born. God was sending Jesus to save us from our sins **(430).** Jesus was sent so that we might know God's love. "For God so loved the world that he gave his only Son, that whoever believes in him should not perish but have eternal life" (John 3:16). Jesus was sent to be our model of holiness as well as **to make us** *"partakers of the divine nature"* (2 Peter 1:4) **(458-460).** We, too, are children of God.

Listen to the beginning of the Prologue of John's Gospel, a hymn that presents the origin and purpose of the Word of God, Jesus, and his mission.

Scripture: Pondering the Word   John 1:1-5, 14

Sharing Question

- How much have I allowed Jesus "to dwell" or "make a home" in me? Is Jesus at the door, in the kitchen, or have I given him the keys to my house?

Exploring the *Catechism* (continued)

Belief in the true Incarnation of the Son of God is the distinctive sign of Christian faith ... (463). The Incarnation does not mean that Jesus is part God and part human, nor does it mean that he is a mixture of the divine and the human. Rather, the Incarnation is the mystery that in Jesus, God became truly human while remaining truly God. **Jesus Christ is true God and true man (464).**

THE WORD BECAME FLESH AND DWELT AMONG US.
JOHN 1.14

This mystery sometimes has been challenged. The first heresies denied either the humanity or the divinity of Christ. One heresy regarded Jesus as a human person joined to the divine person of God's Son. Another heresy **affirmed that the human** nature had ceased to exist as such in Christ when the divine person of God's Son assumed it (465-468). Yet the Church is clear: ... **Jesus is inseparably truly divine and truly human (469).**

The divine name, "I Am" or "He Is," expresses God's faithfulness .... By giving his life to free us from sin, Jesus reveals that he himself bears the divine name: "When you have lifted up the Son of man, then you will realize that 'I Am'" (John 8:28) **(211).** Throughout John's Gospel, we find numerous times where Jesus uses the "I Am" statement revealing his intimate union with the Father. **Very often in the Gospels, people address Jesus as "Lord." This title testifies to the respect and trust of those who approach him for help and healing** (cf. Matthew 8:2; 14:30; 15:22; *et al.*). **At the prompting of the Holy Spirit, "Lord" expresses the recognition of the divine mystery of Jesus** (cf. Luke 1:43; 2:11) **(448).**

Throughout his public life, he [Jesus] **demonstrated his divine sovereignty by works of power over nature, illnesses, demons, death, and sin (447).** The Father's loving concern sent Jesus to be our Lord and Savior, redeeming us.

In his humanity, Jesus has a human body and soul, as we do. Vatican II explained: **"The Son of God ... worked with human hands; he thought with a human mind. He acted with a human will, and with a human heart, he loved. Born of the Virgin Mary, he has truly been made one of us, like us in all things except sin"** (*Gaudium et spes* 22 § 2) **(470).** In his humanity, Jesus had human knowledge, which he exercised in the historical conditions of his existence. He had a human soul, which is why he grew in wisdom and knowledge. He would have to learn as we all do, from the ordinary experience of his life. He ate, slept, and cried, and finally humbled himself even to the point of death **(472).**

"The human nature of God's Son, *not by itself but by its union with the Word*, **knew and showed forth in itself everything that pertains to God"** (St. Maximus the Confessor) **(473).** As a Divine Person, Jesus had a unique, intimate and immediate knowledge of God. Jesus, **in his human knowledge also showed the divine penetration he had into the secret thoughts of human hearts (473). Jesus knew and loved us each and all during his life ....** Jesus **loved us all with a human heart (478).**

The Father chose a unique and loving manner for Jesus to be born into this world. The angel Gabriel announced to Mary, a grace-filled woman, that she was to become the Mother of God through the power of the Holy Spirit.

Against all human expectation God chooses those who were considered powerless and weak to show forth his faithfulness to his promises (489).

The Lord chose Mary who was indeed filled with grace, and responded in faith, knowing "with God nothing will be impossible" (Luke 1:37) **(494).**

As we reflect on the Incarnation, we again reflect on a mystery—the mystery of the wonderful union of the divine and human natures in the one person of the Word. Because of this beautiful union, we can truly say that God has shared his life with us and we, as human beings, have shared ours with God.

Sharing Our Faith

- While the Incarnation is a mystery, we believe in a balance between understanding Jesus as both human and divine. How do I relate to Jesus who is both human and divine?
- How is Jesus a model of holiness for us? What in Jesus' life do I wish to imitate?
- It is said that the face of God is seen through the character of Jesus. How do I describe the face of God as it relates to my experiences with Jesus? What favorite Scripture passage defines the character of Jesus and face of God?
- Mary said a complete "yes" to God. How can I follow her example?

Living the Good News

Determine a specific action (individual or group) that flows from your sharing. This should be your primary consideration.

When choosing an individual action, determine what you will do and share it with the group. When choosing a group action, determine who will take responsibility for different aspects of the action.

The following are secondary suggestions:

- Pray the rosary, reflecting on the Joyful Mysteries.
- Make a visit to the Blessed Sacrament.
- Identify a person in your life who "has the heart of Jesus." Visit or write a letter to this person, and share your love for Jesus with that person.

- Invite someone to pray a Hail Mary with you each day at noontime.
- Between Seasons of *Why Catholic?* you may want to use the appropriate cycle of PRAYERTIME: *Faith-Sharing Reflections on the Sunday Gospels*, Cycle A, B, or C. (For information, see page 78.)

As my response to the gospel of Jesus, this week I commit to _____

_____ .

Lifting Our Hearts

Pray together

>Come, O come, Emmanuel, we pray,
>we need you with us right now, at this time, in this day.
>Drop down dew from heaven,
>that God might walk and talk among us,
>might bring the dew to our parched and dried up earth.
>
>You came in your Incarnation, to be one of us.
>The world had waited long for your coming,
>for the promise that was foretold–
>Wonder Counselor, Mighty God, Eternal Father, Prince of Peace–
>that the gentle lamb would live with the lion.
>
>Come, O come, Emmanuel, we continue to pray.
>We await your coming with peace and hope.
>As you became one of us, make us aware that peace
>will come only when you emerge in our lives.

To conclude, sing "Angels We Have Heard on High."

Looking Ahead

- Prepare for your next session by prayerfully reading and studying **Session 7, The Public Life of Jesus** and paragraphs 512-570 of the *Catechism*.
- Remember to use RENEWING FAMILY FAITH (see pages 76-77) and its helpful suggestions on how to extend the fruits of your sharing beyond your group, especially to your families.

Session 7

The Public Life of Jesus

✝✝✝

Suggested environment

Bible, candle, and, if possible, the *Catechism of the Catholic Church*
Begin with a quiet, reflective atmosphere.

Lifting Our Hearts

Song

"Come to the Water," John Foley, S.J. (OCP)

Pray together

We believe, O Jesus,
that you are the Son of God.
We believe that you redeemed us.
We believe you were like us in all things
except sin.
We know you reached out to sinners,
to the alienated, to the frightened, to the oppressed,
to the sick and dying,
to the helpless,
to all who needed you.
We, too, Jesus, are children of God.
We ask you to teach us
how to live in right relationship.
We ask you to strengthen us
with your love and grace,
So that we will have the courage to emulate you
in all things.
Send forth your Spirit,
and help us to respond
by recognizing what true justice really means.
This we ask of you,
together with the Father and the Holy Spirit,
one God, for ever and ever. Amen.

Sharing Our Good News

*Share how you did with your **Living the Good News** from the previous session.*

Exploring the *Catechism*

Who is this person Jesus? We know that he was both human and divine. Yet who was this Jesus as he lived and walked on this earth? **Almost nothing is said about his hidden life at Nazareth, and even a great part of his public life is not recounted (514).** Yet we do know a lot about Jesus and everything that has been written down in the gospels is given to us so that we might believe and have life in Jesus' name **(514).** All the mysteries of Jesus' life reflect **"God's love ... among us"** (1 John 4:9) **(516).**

Jesus was sent by his Father to show us how to live and to love and in so doing, he was nailed to a cross. He did not come in a lofty manner as a great ruler or king, but rather as a humble servant who endured the cross. Jesus came to be *our model*. He gave **us an example to imitate, through his prayer ... and ... his poverty (520).**

Jesus' public life begins with his baptism by John ... (535-537). Right after Jesus was baptized, he entered the desert and was tempted three times by Satan. These were basic human temptations, temptations to power, possessions, and prestige **(538-540).** After his forty days in the desert, Jesus returned in the power of the Holy Spirit and proclaimed his mission. Listen to the following passage from the Gospel of Luke.

Scripture: Pondering the Word   Luke 4:14-21

Sharing Question

- How have I experienced the healing and forgiving mission of Jesus in my life? How have I been an instrument of Jesus' mission of bringing hope, healing, and comfort to others?

Jesus is Lord and Savior. **By attributing to Jesus the divine title "Lord," the first confessions of the Church's faith affirm from the beginning that the power, honor, and glory due to God the Father are due also to Jesus, because "he was in the form of God," and the Father manifested the sovereignty of Jesus by raising him from the dead and exalting him into his glory** (cf. Romans 10:9; 1 Corinthians 12:3; Philippians 2:9-11) **(449)**. Jesus' divine redemptive mission was expressed in his human love and compassion for all.

His character and teachings were so attractive that people were constantly following him. They were amazed not only at what he did, but at how he spoke and the way he lived. Although Jesus was loving and forgiving toward those who were needy, sick, and repentant, he was challenging to those who were haughty and self-righteous. So often in the Scriptures, we hear that Jesus went away to a lonely place to pray. Jesus' goodness flowed from his relationship with his loving Father. Jesus taught us to depend on God and place our trust in the Father as he did.

A key theme in both the life and teaching of Jesus is the concept of the reign or the kingdom of God. Entering the reign of God is about a new relationship, a growing recognition that we are people who are loved by God and are called to respond to that love. Jesus proclaimed that everyone is called to enter the reign of God **(543)**, that everyone is called to that loving relationship, not only at some future time, but also right now. **"[T]he kingdom of God is at hand"** (Mark 1:15) **(541). To enter it, one must first accept Jesus' word: "The word of the Lord is compared to a seed which is sown in a field; those who hear it with faith and are numbered among the little flock of Christ have truly received the kingdom. Then, by its own power, the seed sprouts and grows until the harvest"** (*Lumen gentium* 5; cf. Mark 4:14, 26-29; Luke 12:32) **(543).**

Jesus' words were often about love and forgiveness. When Jesus raised the person who was paralyzed, his intimate relationship to God became crystal clear to those who had open minds and hearts. But some still refused to believe. Jesus addressed the scribes, "Which is easier, to say to the paralytic, 'Your sins are forgiven,' or to say, 'Rise, take up your mat and walk'?" (Mark 2:10).

Jesus told us that [t]he kingdom belongs *to the poor and the lowly,* **which means those who have accepted it with humble hearts. ... Jesus shares the life of the poor, from the cradle to the cross; he experiences hunger, thirst, and privation. Jesus identifies himself with the poor of every kind and makes active love toward them the condition for entering his kingdom (544). Jesus invites** *sinners* **to the table of the kingdom .... He invites them to that conversion without which one cannot enter the kingdom ....** He reminds so many he meets that God's love and mercy are boundless **(545).**

Many times Jesus' words come in the form of parables. Parables are stories or metaphors that communicate a particular point. Jesus used metaphors that came from the experience of the ordinary life of the people. The reign of God is like a mustard seed. The reign of God is like a pearl of great price. **Through his parables [Jesus] invites people to the feast of the kingdom, but he also asks for a radical choice: to gain the kingdom, one must give everything. Words are not enough; deeds are required. The parables are like mirrors ... : will [we] be hard soil or good earth for the word?** Jesus and the presence of the kingdom in this world are at the heart of the parables. We must **enter the kingdom, that is, become ... disciple[s] of Christ, in order to "know the secrets of the kingdom of heaven"** (Matthew 13:11) **(546).** Jesus' parables challenged not only the people of his time, but they challenge and instruct us today.

Jesus accompanies his words with many "mighty works and wonders and signs" ... (547). The miracles that Jesus performed **invite belief in him**. People came to believe that Jesus was one who does God's works. People were fascinated by his miracles, but he performed them not **to satisfy** [their] **curiosity or desire for magic**, but out of his compassion to cure people and to convince them of his divinity. His miracles gave powerful testimony to the fact that Jesus is the Son of God **(548).**

"The whole of Christ's life was a continual teaching: his silences, his miracles, his gestures, his prayer, his love for people, his special affection for the little and the poor, his acceptance of the total sacrifice on the

Cross for the redemption of the world, and his Resurrection ..." (John Paul II, *Catechesi Tradendae* 9) **(561)**. We learn from Jesus how to be loving and forgiving, how to look to God for all our needs, how to become humble and open. We learn that God is trustworthy and that we can put our life completely in his hands. From Jesus, we come to know God because Jesus is the complete and total revelation of God. If we look at the life of Jesus, we find a person who is a model of love, our Savior and Redeemer.

Sharing Our Faith

- What motivates me to put my faith in Jesus?
- How would I respond to the question Jesus asked his disciples, "Who do you say that I am?" Who is Jesus to me? Why do I believe in him?
- What favorite gospel story helps me understand who Jesus is?
- How does the reality of Jesus as our Savior affect my life and our society?

Living the Good News

Determine a specific action (individual or group) that flows from your sharing. This should be your primary consideration.

When choosing an individual action, determine what you will do and share it with the group. When choosing a group action, determine who will take responsibility for different aspects of the action.

The following are secondary suggestions:

- Write a letter to Jesus to tell him of your love.
- Make a commitment to read and pray the Scriptures each day.
- Meet someone who is poor and needy and respond to that person's need.
- Express your gratitude that you have been called to faith by the Church, which continues its mission to make Christ present among us.

As my response to the gospel of Jesus, this week I commit to _____

_____.

Lifting Our Hearts

Leader: If possible, give small candles to each person to hold during this time of prayer. Light one candle and invite people to pass the light on to others. Ask three individuals to read the following Images of Light:

1. "I am the light of the world. Whoever follows me will never walk in darkness but will have the light of life" (John 8:12).

2. "We must work the works of him who sent me while it is day; night is coming when no one can work. As long as I am in the world, I am the light of the world" (John 9:4, 5).

3. "You are the light of the world. A city built on a hill cannot be hid. No one after lighting a lamp puts it under the bushel basket, but on the lampstand, and it gives light to all in the house. In the same way, let your light shine before others, so that they may see your good works and give glory to your Father in heaven" (Matthew 5:14-16).

(prayed alternately by two people or two groups)

Side 1	Arise, shine; for your light has come, and the glory of the LORD has risen upon you. For darkness shall cover the earth, and thick darkness the peoples; *(Isaiah 60:1-2a)*
Side 2	but the LORD will arise upon you, and his glory will appear over you. Nations shall come to your light, and kings to the brightness of your dawn. *(Isaiah 60:2b-3)*
Side 1	The sun shall no longer be your light by day, nor for brightness shall the moon give light to you by night; but the LORD will be your everlasting light, and your God will be your glory. *(Isaiah 60:19)*
Side 2	Your sun shall no more go down, or your moon withdraw itself; for the LORD will be your everlasting light, and your days of mourning shall be ended. *(Isaiah 60:20)*
Side 1	... for you are all children of light and children of the day; we are not of the night or of darkness. *(1 Thessalonians 5:5)*
All	... the darkness is passing away and the true light is already shining. *(1 John 2:8)*

For it is God who said,
"Let light shine out of darkness,"
who has shone in our hearts
to give the light of the knowledge of the glory of God
in the face of Jesus Christ. *(2 Corinthians 4:6)*

Looking Ahead

- Prepare for your next session by prayerfully reading and studying **Session 8, The Paschal Mystery: Jesus' Death and Resurrection** and paragraphs 571-682 of the *Catechism*.

- Remember to use *RENEWING FAMILY FAITH* (see pages 76-77) and its helpful suggestions on how to extend the fruits of your sharing beyond your group, especially to your families.

Session 8

The Paschal Mystery:
Jesus' Death and Resurrection

†††

Suggested environment

Bible, candle, and, if possible, the *Catechism of the Catholic Church*
Begin with a quiet, reflective atmosphere.

Lifting Our Hearts

Song

"We Remember," Marty Haugen (GIA)

Pray together

We praise you, God our Father, for the total outpouring
     of your love to us in and through Jesus Christ.
We remember his suffering and death—
     the Paschal Mystery that we, too, are called to live.
May we remember his life, his love, and his sacrifice,
     so that we become strong in imitating his life,
     courageous in loving the unloved and unlovable,
     willing to overcome any unwillingness to forgive,
     and to defend the oppressed and those who suffer from injustice.
May we be conscious of his living presence with us,
     because you raised him up from the grip of death and the tomb.
May his Resurrection give us hope
     to continue our journey with greater confidence
     and thus fulfill the mission he has given us:
     to be his witnesses to the whole world.
We surrender ourselves to you
     in the unity of the Holy Trinity, now and for ever. Amen.

Sharing Our Good News
*Share how you did with your **Living the Good News** from the previous session.*

Exploring the *Catechism*

The Paschal mystery ... stands at the center of the Good News that the apostles, and the Church following them, are to proclaim to the world (571). The Paschal mystery has two aspects: by his death, Christ liberates us from sin; by his Resurrection, he opens for us the way to a new life (654).

We know that from the beginning of Jesus' life, and especially his public ministry, certain leaders were trying to destroy him. He was accused of blasphemy and false prophecy as well as religious crimes **(574).** Jesus was a "sign of contradiction" (Luke 2:34) for some of the religious leaders in Jerusalem **(575). Jesus seems to be acting against essential institutions ...: the Law in its written commandments...; the centrality of the Temple at Jerusalem ...; their faith in the one God ... (576).** Jesus confronted the leaders and teachers who were responsible for interpreting the Law and maintaining the Temple. He pointed out that some of them had twisted God's gifts for personal gain and judged others in a hypocritical manner.

Jesus fulfilled the Law perfectly, but he often offended **the teachers of the Law, for he was not content to propose his interpretation alongside theirs but taught the people "as one who had authority, and not as their scribes"** (Matthew 7:28-29) **(581).** Jesus did not destroy the Law; he fulfilled it **(577).** Jesus did not ignore the Temple; he had a deep respect for the Temple **(583). Jesus scandalized the Pharisees by eating with tax collectors and sinners ...** (cf. Luke 5:30; 7:36; 11:37; 14:1). He upset them when he showed his merciful conduct toward sinners. He was seen as blaspheming when he made himself God's equal or was speaking the truth.

It was, in fact, **his role in the redemption of sins ... [that] was the true stumbling-block** (cf. Luke 2:34; 20:17-18; Psalm 118:22) for the religious authorities **(587-589).** Many of the leaders of the Temple at that time were so afraid that all they could think to do was to get rid of this person who called them to be something more than they were.

Scripture: Pondering the Word   Mark 8:27-38

Sharing Question

- In this reading we hear that Jesus will suffer, die, and rise again. How have I experienced new growth and life out of times of loss, disappointment, or death?

Exploring the *Catechism* (continued)

The Paschal mystery of Christ's cross and Resurrection stands at the center of the Good News that the apostles, and the Church following them, are to proclaim to the world. God's saving plan was accomplished "once for all" by the redemptive death of his Son Jesus Christ (571).

Jesus shared our human nature, as is clear in his prayer in Gethsemane, when he prayed, "Father, let this cup pass from me, but not my will, yours be done" (Matthew 26:39). Jesus was afraid, yet willing to do God's will. How many times we also experience the same fears, but if we follow Jesus, we will be able to say, "Your will be done."

In his divinity, Jesus was sent to fulfill his mission, the redemption of the human family. Just as the blood of the lamb smeared on their doorposts had saved the people of Israel from the angel of death, who was destroying the firstborn of the Egyptians, so the blood of Jesus poured out for us saves us from eternal death. Jesus is **"the Lamb of God, who takes away the sin of the world," and the *sacrifice of the New Covenant*, which restores man to communion with God by reconciling him to God through the "blood of the covenant, which was poured out for many for the forgiveness of sins" (613).**

The life, suffering, death, and Resurrection of Christ are at the center of God's long history of salvation. **From the first moment of his Incarnation the Son embraces the Father's plan of divine salvation in his redemptive mission: "My food is to do the will of him who sent me, and to accomplish his work"** (John 4:34). **The sacrifice of Jesus "for the sins of the whole world"** (1 John 2:2) **expresses his loving communion with the Father. "The Father loves me, because I lay down my life,"** said the Lord, **"[for] I do as the Father has commanded me, so that the world may know that I love the Father"** (John 10:17, 14:31) **(606).**

This sacrifice of Christ is unique; it completes and surpasses all other sacrifices. First, it is a gift from God the Father himself, for the Father handed his Son over to sinners in order to reconcile us with himself. At the same time it is the offering of the Son of God made man, who in freedom and love offered his life to his Father through the Holy Spirit in reparation for our disobedience (614).

The Father *gave* us his only Son, and Jesus *gave up* his life in order to show love for us, a love that is benevolent and not based on any of our own merit **(604). Our Church teaches us that Christ died for** all, **without exception: "There is not, never has been, and never will be a single human being for whom Christ did not suffer"** (Council of Quiercy, [853]) **(605).** While we know Jesus struggled to respond to God's will in his suffering and dying, he was willing to embrace his Father's loving plan **(571);** in fact, Jesus knew this **was the very reason for his Incarnation (607). Indeed, out of love, Jesus freely accepted his passion and death: "No one takes it from me, but I lay it down of my own accord"** (John 10:18) **(609).**

We are partners in the Paschal Mystery. **The cross is the unique sacrifice of Christ,** yet we, too, participate in it since Jesus united himself to all of us. We, too, are called to take up our cross and follow Jesus. St. Rose of Lima said so clearly: **"Apart from the cross there is no other ladder by which we may get to heaven"** (cf. P. Hansen, *Vita mirabilis*) **(618).** What a powerful symbol the cross is for us as we enter into our own suffering. While sometimes the mystery of the cross is difficult to understand, there is probably no greater help to those suffering than to know that Jesus, too, experienced terrible suffering and death.

We learn from the Paschal Mystery the balance between death and new life. Jesus rises above sin and death, and invites and enables us to do the same. We all experience many small deaths, and we will each experience physical death. We are called to join with Jesus and accept suffering, pain, and finally death in order to enter into new life.

Jesus' redemptive acceptance of his crucifixion, death, and Resurrection empower us to die and rise with him. Suffering in faith can help us enter into a loving, deep relationship with Jesus.

As Christians, we believe, and through our Baptism participate, not only in the death of Jesus but also his Resurrection. **The mystery of Christ's resurrection is a real event, with manifestations that were historically verified, as the New Testament bears witness (639).**

Mary Magdalene and the holy women were the first to see the risen Jesus. While it was difficult for Peter and the disciples to believe, once they saw Jesus, they, too became witnesses to his Resurrection **(641-642)**. Jesus establishes himself again with his disciples through sharing a meal. He invites them to recognize that he is not a ghost, but that he has a real body with the special properties of a glorified body **(645)**.

To believe in Jesus' Resurrection requires faith in **a transcendent intervention of God ... in creation and history (648). ... Christ's Resurrection is the fulfillment of the promises both of the Old Testament and of Jesus himself during his earthly life (652). ... The truth of Jesus' divinity is confirmed by his Resurrection (653). ... Christ's Resurrection ... is the principle and source of our future resurrection (655).**

Sharing Our Faith

- How have I experienced suffering in my life? In what ways did it bring me to new life? How did I experience God's grace in the midst of my pain?
- How do I confront darkness or selfishness in my life? How can we claim the victory of Jesus who redeemed us from our sins?
- Who are the people I know or have heard about who are suffering today? What can I do to help them?
- How do we experience the Resurrection in our world today?

Living the Good News

Determine a specific action (individual or group) that flows from your sharing. This should be your primary consideration.

When choosing an individual action, determine what you will do and share it with the group. When choosing a group action, determine who will take responsibility for different aspects of the action.

The following are secondary suggestions:

- Pray the Stations of the Cross. As you do, recall and pray about contemporary situations that come to mind as you reflect on each event of Jesus' life.
- Reach out to someone who is suffering and offer your support and love. In other words, help someone carry his or her cross.
- Visit someone in a hospital or nursing home.
- Celebrate with your group or with someone who has experienced new life.

As my response to the gospel of Jesus, this week I commit to _____

_____ .

Lifting Our Hearts

Sing again the Opening Song, "We Remember."

Pray together

"Father, …
I ask not only on behalf of these,
but also on behalf of those
who will believe in me through their word,
that they may all be one.
As you, Father, are in me and I am in you,
may they also be in us,
so that the world may believe that you have sent me.
The glory that you have given me
I have given them,
so that they may be one,
as we are one,
I in them and you in me,

so that they may become completely one,
so that the world may know that you have sent me
and have loved them
even as you have loved me" (John 17:20-23).

Looking Ahead

- Prepare for your next session by prayerfully reading and studying **Session 9, The Holy Spirit and the Church** and paragraphs 683-810 of the *Catechism*.

- Remember to use RENEWING FAMILY FAITH (see pages 76-77) and its helpful suggestions on how to extend the fruits of your sharing beyond your group, especially to your families.

Session 9

The Holy Spirit and the Church

✝✝✝

Suggested environment

Bible, candle, and, if possible, the *Catechism of the Catholic Church*
Begin with a quiet, reflective atmosphere.

Lifting Our Hearts

Song

"Send Us Your Spirit," David Haas (OCP)

Pray together

> Come, Holy Spirit, fill the hearts of your faithful
> and enkindle in them the fire of your love.
>
> Send forth your Spirit
> and they shall be created
> and you shall renew the face of the earth.
>
> Holy Spirit, we need you.
> Come to us and renew us.
> Give us the grace
> to be attentive to your inspirations,
> and to respond to your prompting.
> Help us remember
> that the true marks of your presence
> are love, joy, peace, patience, kindness,
> generosity, faithfulness,
> gentleness, and self-control. *(Galatians 5:22, 23)*
> We ask this through Christ our Lord. Amen.

Sharing Our Good News

*Share how you did with your **Living the Good News** from the previous session.*

Exploring the *Catechism*

"Holy Spirit" is the proper name of the third person of the Trinity, the one whom we adore and glorify with God the Father and God the Son. **The term "Spirit" translates the Hebrew word *ruah*, which, in its primary sense, means breath, air, wind (691).** We believe that our very breathing is the movement of the Holy Spirit. There are so many beautiful symbols we have of the Spirit: water, anointing, fire, cloud and light, the seal, the hand, the finger of God, the dove **(694-701).** All of these symbols reveal God, who is dynamic and full of power.

IT IS THE SPIRIT THAT GIVES LIFE.
JOHN 6.63

We know about the Holy Spirit from Jesus. At his Baptism, the Spirit came upon Jesus. While talking with Nicodemus, Jesus explains that no one can enter into God's reign without first being begotten of water and the Spirit. In John 16, Jesus promises to send the Spirit, and Jesus fulfilled that promise. **On the day of Pentecost when the seven weeks of Easter had come to an end, Christ's Passover is fulfilled in the outpouring of the Holy Spirit ... (731).**

When we say we believe in the Holy Spirit, we are saying that we believe that the Spirit "who has spoken through the prophets" opens us to hear the Word of God. We know the Spirit in the way by which faith is revealed to us. We know the Spirit because the Spirit who dwells in us is the power of God **(687),** and we are invited to participate in that great power. **"The Spirit helps us in our weakness; for we do not know how to pray as we ought, but the Spirit ... intercedes with sighs too deep for words"** (Romans 8:26) **(741).** The Spirit prays through us. We would live much better lives if we kept in our hearts the truth that we are empowered by the Holy Spirit, by the Spirit of God.

Scripture: Pondering the Word   1 Corinthians 2:6-16

Sharing Question

- Jesus promised to send the Holy Spirit who will lead us to all truth (John 14:26). When have I experienced the power of the Holy Spirit in my life?

Christ was filled with the Holy Spirit. **The mission of Christ and the Holy Spirit is brought to completion in the Church, which is the Body of Christ ….** The Spirit *prepares* us and leads us in grace; the Spirit *manifests* the risen Christ to us; the Spirit makes present the mystery of Christ in the Eucharist, and *brings us into communion* with God so that we may "bear much fruit" **(737)**. The mission of the Church **is not an addition to that of Christ and the Holy Spirit, but is its sacrament … the Church is sent to announce, bear witness, make present, and spread the mystery of the communion of the Holy Trinity… (738).** As sacrament, the Church in this world is the sign and instrument of the communion and unity of the whole human race **(775)**.

The word "Church" (Latin *ecclesia*, from the Greek *ek-kalein*, to "call out of") means a convocation or an assembly (751). In Christian usage, the word "church" designates the liturgical assembly, but also the local community or the whole universal community of believers. These three meanings are inseparable. "The Church" is the People that God gathers in the whole world. She exists in local communities and is made real as a liturgical, above all a Eucharistic, assembly. She draws her life from the word and the Body of Christ and so herself becomes Christ's Body (752).

The seven **Sacraments** of the Church **are "powers that come forth" from the Body of Christ …. They are actions of the Holy Spirit at work in … the Church** (cf. Luke 5:17; 6:19; 8:46) **(1116)**.

"What the soul is to the human body, the Holy Spirit is to the Body of Christ, which is the Church" (St. Augustine, *Enarrationes in Psalmos* 74:4) **(797).** The Spirit dwells in and guides the community that we call the Church. The Spirit dwells in the entire body and not just in individuals. The Spirit works in many ways to build up the whole body. The Spirit provides graces or charisms that benefit the Church and the needs of the world. Each of us receives gifts of the Holy Spirit that are to be used for the good of all **(799-800)**.

In the early Church, those who were called to be disciples of Jesus saw themselves as a community united in love and led by the Spirit of God. These early Christians believed they were united to one another by the power of the Holy Spirit who formed them into a community and called them to proclaim the good news that Jesus had lived, died, and had risen from the dead. At Pentecost, the Holy Spirit set their hearts on fire and enabled them to draw many new believers into this community of faith and love.

In fact, the Holy Spirit is at the center of the Church's mission. **"When the work which the Father gave the Son to do on earth was accomplished, the Holy Spirit was sent on the day of Pentecost in order that he might continually sanctify the Church"** (*Lumen gentium* 4). Then **"the Church was openly displayed to the crowds and the spread of the Gospel among the nations, through preaching, was begun"** (*Ad gentes* 4). As the **"convocation"** of all men for salvation, the Church in her very nature is missionary, sent by Christ to all the nations to make disciples of them (*Ad gentes* 2; 5-6) **(767)**.

So that she can fulfill her mission, the Holy Spirit **"bestows upon [the Church] varied hierarchic and charismatic gifts, and in this way directs her"** (*Lumen gentium* 4). **"Henceforward the Church, endowed with the gifts of her founder and faithfully observing his precepts of charity, humility and self-denial, receives the mission of proclaiming and establishing among all peoples the Kingdom of Christ and of God, and she is on earth the seed and the beginning of that kingdom"** (*Lumen gentium* 5) **(768)**.

Like the early Christians, God calls us to recognize the power of the Spirit in the community of faithful, the universal Church. We are called to recognize the Spirit of truth who resides in the body. Through the Spirit, Jesus' spirit is still living and breathing in the body, the community of believers. Not only does the Holy Spirit enable us to believe in Christ and put our hope for eternal salvation in him, but the Spirit also enables us to love one another as Christ loves us. It is here that the moral life finds its source and vitality (see **1971, 1972**).

What a critical question of faith: Do we really believe in Pentecost? Do we really believe that the Spirit dwells in us as Church?

Sharing Our Faith

- How do I see the Holy Spirit acting in the body of believers today?
- What experiences have most helped me understand the Church as a community, inspired and led by the Holy Spirit?

- What charisms or gifts of the Holy Spirit have I been given? How can I use these for the common good?

Living the Good News

Determine a specific action (individual or group) that flows from your sharing. This should be your primary consideration.

When choosing an individual action, determine what you will do and share it with the group. When choosing a group action, determine who will take responsibility for different aspects of the action.

The following are secondary suggestions:

- Read the Acts of the Apostles. Be aware of how the Spirit moved in the early Church.
- Share the good news of God's love for us this week with someone who is struggling with his or her faith.
- Pray for inspiration from the Holy Spirit to be grateful to God for the gift that is the Church.

As my response to the gospel of Jesus, this week I commit to _____

_____.

Lifting Our Hearts

Sing again the Opening Song, "Send Us Your Spirit."

Offer spontaneous prayers followed by the response, "Send us your Spirit, Lord, and we shall be renewed."

Conclude with the Our Father *and the* Glory Be.

Looking Ahead

- Prepare for your next session by prayerfully reading and studying **Session 10, One Church with Diverse Roles** and paragraphs 811-945 of the *Catechism*.
- Remember to use *RENEWING FAMILY FAITH* (see pages 76-77) and its helpful suggestions on how to extend the fruits of your sharing beyond your group, especially to your families.

Session 10
One Church with Diverse Roles

✝✝✝

Suggested environment

Bible, candle, and, if possible, the *Catechism of the Catholic Church*
Begin with a quiet, reflective atmosphere.

Lifting Our Hearts

Song

"Gather Your People, O Lord," Bob Hurd (OCP)

Pray together

Father, we thank you for the gifts of Sacred Scripture and Sacred Tradition
  you have given through your Church.
We thank you for the gifts you have given us
  through the seven sacraments of the Catholic Church.
We thank you also for dwelling within us,
  enabling us to believe in Jesus,
  and to place all our hope in him.
We thank you for helping us to love one another
  by leading good moral lives.
Finally, we thank you for the personal gifts
  you have given to each one of us, your people.
We ask that you teach us to use our gifts in your service.
May we use them for your honor and glory.
May we welcome all people
  with their particular gifts,
  and encourage their use for your glory.
May we never be envious of others' gifts
  but realize that all gifts come from you.
Empower us, sustain us, love us,
  and help us to be faithful
  to all you have given us.
We ask this in Jesus' name. Amen.

Sharing Our Good News

*Share how you did with your **Living the Good News** from the previous session.*

Exploring the *Catechism*

As a community, we pray: We believe in one, holy, catholic, and apostolic Church. These are the four characteristics of the Church and her mission, which Christ, through the ongoing power of the Holy Spirit, calls the Church to realize **(811).**

The Church is one .... **The Church is one** *because of her "soul":* **"It is the Holy Spirit, dwelling in those who believe ... who brings about that wonderful communion of the faithful and joins them together ...** in **unity"** (*Unitatis redintegratio* 2 § 2). **Unity is of the essence of the Church .... (813). The Church is holy:** the Church is the Holy People of God because God created her and **the Spirit of holiness gives her life (867).** The Church is catholic, meaning **"universal" or "in keeping with the whole" (830).** The Church proclaims the fullness of faith to all peoples. The Church is missionary by nature **(849-856).** Finally, **[t]he Church is apostolic because she is founded on the apostles ... (857).** The mission entrusted to them continues through the successors of the apostles **(858). The Church is ultimately** *one, holy, catholic, and apostolic* **... because it is in her that ... the "Reign of God" already exists and will be fulfilled at the end of time (865).**

Listen to Jesus' priestly prayer in which he prays for his disciples and for all who will believe in him through their word.

Scripture: Pondering the Word   John 17:1-26

Sharing Question

- In what ways am I living out the meaning of the prayer of Jesus for unity in my family, neighborhood, and parish community

(John 17:21-22)? In what community (e.g. family, work) do I most need to be an instrument of healing and unity?

Exploring the *Catechism* (continued)

Unity with diversity—what a wonderful gift Jesus left us. All of us as Christian faithful, have been baptized, and thus constitute the people of God. As Christians, we all share in Christ's priestly, prophetic, and royal office, and are all called to exercise the mission God has entrusted to the Church to fulfill Christ's mission **(871).** The *Code of Canon Law* (208), echoing Vatican II, teaches us that there is a **"true equality with regard to dignity and the activity whereby all cooperate in the building up of the Body of Christ"** in their own unique manner **(872).** The Catholic Church is composed of laity, religious, and clergy. There is a difference in roles, but not in the value of those roles. The differences between members of the body are meant to **serve its unity and mission**, not to create division or levels of importance in the eyes of God **(873).**

If we look back to the early Church, we see the unique leadership of Peter, the first pope. Jesus said, "You are Peter, and upon this rock I will build my church …" (Matthew 16:18). **This pastoral office of Peter and the other apostles belongs to the Church's very foundation and is continued by the bishops** today **(881).** The *Pope*, **Bishop of Rome and Peter's successor, "is the perpetual and visible source and foundation of the unity both of the bishops and of the whole company of the faithful"** (*Lumen gentium* 23) **(882).** The primacy of the pope is a primacy of service. He is not just the Bishop of Rome, but also the Bishop of the universal Church.

"The individual *bishops* are the visible source and foundation of unity in their own particular Churches" (*Lumen gentium* 23) **(886).** From these individual Churches comes the universal Church. The bishops, with the pope, have the threefold responsibility for teaching, sanctifying, and governing or leading the Church **(888-896).** When the college of bishops gathers in an ecumenical council, it exercises power within the universal Church in a solemn manner, but this is never done without the leadership of the pope. As a college of bishops, there is the expression of the variety and the universality of the people of God **(884-885)**—again, unity in diversity.

What is the role of men called to priesthood? Jesus entrusted a unique role of leadership to those in authority in the believing community. The priest is the steward of the mysteries of faith. He has a ministry of proclaiming and preaching the Word. Its character as service is intrinsically linked to the sacramental nature of ecclesial ministry. The priest has a sacramental ministry, making Christ present in power and in mercy through the seven signs he has given to the Catholic Church. In the liturgy of the Eucharist, the priest acts *in persona Christi*—in the person of Jesus himself, making present the unique sacrifice of Christ for the salvation of the world. He feeds us with the Body and Blood of our Lord. Apart from the community, no one is given the mandate and the mission to proclaim the gospel. Only Christ and the community of the Church can bestow this sacred power **(875).** Jesus was a servant to all, and ecclesial ministry demands a life of service for the good of the Church and the good of all **(876).** In addition, those called to ecclesial ministry are called to collegial ministry. Jesus chose the Twelve and they were sent out together. [T]heir **... unity would be at the service of the ... communion of all the faithful ... (877).** Finally, those called to priesthood are to be pastoral, to care for the needs of parishioners or those they serve.

LOVE ONE ANOTHER

AS I HAVE LOVED YOU. John 15:12

The lay faithful have a unique role in participating in the reign of God. Together with priests, bishops, and the pope, they participate in the saving mission of the Church. They have the responsibility **by virtue of their Baptism and Confirmation ... to work so that the divine message of salvation may be known and accepted by all (900).** The laity have a particular call to witness to the mission of Jesus in the public square—as they minister in their families, in their places of business, in their neighborhoods, in all areas of society. **The initiative of lay Christians is necessary especially when the matter involves discovering or inventing the means for permeating social, political, and economic realities with the demands of Christian doctrine and life (899).**

Lay people are becoming more involved in participating in Church structures and are called to minister within the Church itself **(903).** They, too, have a proper role in the Church's threefold mission. They strive to adhere to the will of God and give an example to all of Christian discipleship. The holiness of their lives is a direct response to the Catholic Church's call to sanctify the world. In order for lay members of the Christian faithful to cooperate further in the exercise of governance, they are encouraged to participate in particular councils, diocesan synods, pastoral councils, finance councils, etc. **(911).** Like the clergy, the laity are called to fulfill their prophetic mission by evangelization, that is, by proclaiming the Good News of Jesus in all aspects of their lives **(905).**

The Lord calls all the faithful to a life consecrated to the evangelical counsels of poverty, chastity, and obedience. God calls certain members of the Church, however, to profess these counsels within a permanent state. Persons called to live as sisters and brothers in community are a sign and symbol. They publicly profess that the reign of God is here and now.

The Holy Spirit has bestowed wonderful charisms upon our Catholic Church. Each religious community has a particular gift to offer the Church and the world: some contemplation, others service; some teaching, others hospitality; some love for the poor, others compassion and healing. All offer gifts of the Spirit to show the world how wonderfully God acts in our world **(931).** Those who accept the call to religious life offer encouragement to all the faithful and **bear striking witness "that the world cannot be transfigured and offered to God without the spirit of the Beatitudes"** (*Lumen gentium* 31 § 2) **(932).**

What a beautiful unity and communion God has created and is creating in the Catholic Church. The faithful on earth, the souls in purgatory, the saints in heaven make up the communion of saints. **The communion of saints is the Church (946).** Saint Thomas Aquinas tells us **"[s]ince all the faithful form one body, the good of each is communicated to the others .... We must therefore believe that there exists a communion of goods in the Church. But the most important member is Christ, since he is the head .... Therefore, the riches of Christ are communicated to all the members through the sacraments"** (St. Thomas Aquinas, *Expositio in symbolum apostolicum,* 10). **"As this Church is governed by one and the same Spirit, all the goods she has received necessarily become a common fund"** (Roman *Catechism* I, 10, 24) **(947).**

The sacraments are powerful signs of Christ's abiding and dynamic presence in the life of the Catholic faithful. His grace reconciles the world to his Father and enables us to love one another as he taught. In the sacraments, Jesus makes us members of his own family, forgives us our sins, and draws us into an ever more intimate union with the divine persons. **[The] sacraments are ... links uniting the faithful with one another and bind-**

ing them to Jesus Christ … Baptism is the gate by which we enter into the Church. … The name "communion" can be applied to all of [the sacraments], for they unite us to God …. But this name is better suited to the Eucharist than to any other, because it is primarily the Eucharist that brings this communion about (Roman *Catechism* I, 10, 24) **(950).**

Sharing Our Faith

- How do I understand my call as a disciple of Jesus Christ? What gifts has God given me to live this discipleship?
- What has been my experience of the positive gifts of priests? Of the laity? Of those in religious life?
- What concrete things can I do to help my parish members become more united to one another and to Christ?

Living the Good News

Determine a specific action (individual or group) that flows from your sharing. This should be your primary consideration.

When choosing an individual action, determine what you will do and share it with the group. When choosing a group action, determine who will take responsibility for different aspects of the action.

The following are secondary suggestions:

- If you are a priest or bishop, affirm the gifts of a layperson. If you are a layperson, affirm the gifts of a priest or bishop.
- Share the Good News of Jesus with someone who is not familiar with Jesus.
- If you are not involved in your parish, volunteer to become a greeter or respond to a needed ministry.

As my response to the gospel of Jesus, this week I commit to _____

_____ .

Lifting Our Hearts

The leader reads slowly 1 Corinthians 12:1-11. The leader then asks members to pray spontaneously about the gifts he or she possesses, or the gifts he or she sees in someone else in the parish or in the group. These are prayers of thanksgiving.

Example:
I thank you, God, for the gift of openness, which I see in our pastor.
May you bless him and continue to allow this gift to grow.

When all have had the opportunity to pray, the leader then says:

In thanksgiving for all the gifts God has placed in our parish,
let us pray together in the words that Jesus taught us:
Our Father, …

To conclude, offer each other a sign of God's peace.

Looking Ahead

- Prepare for your next session by prayerfully reading and studying **Session 11, Mary, Mother of Jesus, Mother of the Church** and paragraphs 946-975 of the *Catechism*.
- Remember to use *RENEWING FAMILY FAITH* (see pages 76-77) and its helpful suggestions on how to extend the fruits of your sharing beyond your group, especially to your families.

Session 11

Mary, Mother of Christ, Mother of the Church

✝✝✝

Suggested environment

Bible, candle, and if possible, a statue or picture of the Blessed Mother and the *Catechism of the Catholic Church*
Begin with a quiet, reflective atmosphere.

Lifting Our Hearts

Song

"Holy Mystery," Tim Hosman (White Dove Productions/OCP/RENEW)

Or sing together another song to Mary.

Pray together

> Mary of Nazareth,
>> beloved of God,
>> model of faith,
>> bearer of God's Word,
>>> you bring truth to light.
>
> Responding to the stirring within,
>> you reach out in compassion
>> to all you encounter,
>> gently encouraging us
>> to become the people of peace
>> we were created to be.
>
> Mother of Christ, Mother of the Church,
>> pray for us that we, too,
>> may be alive in Christ's love
>> for our sisters and brothers. Amen.

Exploring the *Catechism*

After we proclaim that we are one holy catholic and apostolic Church, we add that we believe in "the communion of saints" **(946).** Since all the faithful form one body, we believe there exists a **... communion "in holy things (***sancta***)" and "among holy persons (***sancti***)" (948).** Those who have gone before us and have lived holy lives are very much alive to us today, and we are able to be in communion with them. They can indeed be our good friends. We can learn from them; we can learn how to put God in the center of our lives. We are truly one family in God's love.

Mary, the mother of Jesus Christ and the mother of the Church, has a very special role in our lives. By her willing- ness and complete adherence to the Father's will, by participating in the redemptive work of Jesus, and by lis- tening to every prompting of the Holy Spirit, **Mary is the Church's model of faith and charity (967).** She listened to the stirrings in her heart and responded with complete love. While she may have been frightened or unclear about her call to become God's mother, she allowed his life to be born within her and nurtured that life. Listen to Mary's words of "fiat," her "yes" to God.

Scripture: Pondering the Word   Luke 1:26-38

Sharing Question

- How is Mary's "yes" to God's call an inspiration and model for me to respond to God's will in my life?

Exploring the *Catechism* (continued)

Who is this person, Mary? Who is Mary for us today? We know she is the mother of God, but do we also know she was a very faithful and spirit-filled woman?

Mary's "yes" was an act of complete obedience to God's will. In the beginning when the angel Gabriel came to her, Mary willingly proclaimed: "I am the servant of the Lord. Let it be done to me as you say" (cf. Luke 1:38). What a strong woman, a woman able to be completely open to God, a woman full of grace, a woman who understood that her power came from the mighty power of God. Mary not only understood that his power was to become manifest in her, but she, like Jesus, challenges some of the basic attitudes of our society. She understands from the beginning that the Father chose her to "confuse the proud," that God chose her to "depose the mighty and raise the lowly" (cf. Luke 1:51, 52). He chose her as an instrument to recognize that the hungry would be fed and the rich sent away empty. The Annunciation not only revealed that Jesus would be born, but also who Jesus would be in this world.

So often in the Scriptures, we see Mary in relationship with others. After the angel's visit, one of the first things Mary did was make a very long journey to visit her cousin, Elizabeth. Elizabeth was for Mary a mentor, someone who helped Mary understand her gift of complete faith in God's will. Elizabeth proclaimed to Mary: "Blest is she who trusted that the Lord's words to her would be fulfilled" (cf. Luke 1:45). These two women of God, these women of wisdom, recognized God who was within them.

Because Mary is the mother of Jesus who is the Son of God, Mary is the Mother of God. Mary's **role in relation to the Church and to all humanity goes still further**. We recognize her today as the mother of the Church. She cooperated by her obedience, faith, hope, and charity in the work of salvation; thus she has also become mother to all of us. We call her Advocate and Helper **(968-969).** We offer great devotion to Mary in prayer and reverence. **"The Church's devotion to the Blessed Virgin is intrinsic to Christian worship"** (Paul VI, *Marialis cultus*, 56). **The Church rightly honors "the Blessed Virgin with special devotion"** (*Lumen gentium* 66) **(971).** The liturgical feasts dedicated to Mary and Marian prayer, such as the rosary, express our devotion to Mary who is our mother **(971).**

We have beautiful icons and symbols of Mary. Many of us look to Mary in times of need, especially when we desire the healing presence of a loving mother. We are beginning to understand more and more the power that Mary had, not because of her own doing, but because she was indeed the first disciple of Jesus. She was at the foot of the cross and suffered deeply with her son. She was with the disciples at Pentecost. Mary carried her convictions and beliefs, but more importantly, her unconditional love to the world. Today we acknowledge Mary's "blessedness" and reaffirm what Mary knew: *"All generations will call me blessed"* (Luke 1:48) **(971).**

Sharing Our Faith

- What are my favorite images of Mary? Why do I like them? How do I honor Mary?
- How is Mary "blessed" to this generation?
- How is Mary a model for us today?
- What can I learn from Mary about being a disciple? How will I go about deepening my discipleship with Jesus through Mary?

Living the Good News

Determine a specific action (individual or group) that flows from your sharing. This should be your primary consideration.

When choosing an individual action, determine what you will do and share it with the group. When choosing a group action, determine who will take responsibility for different aspects of the action.

The following are secondary suggestions:

- Pray the rosary during the coming week.
- Read a book on the lives of the saints. Pray to your favorite or write in your journal about this saint.
- Learn about the FIAT Rosary and make a commitment to pray it. *(Information on the FIAT Rosary can be found on the website: www.fiat-spiritualityusa.com)*

- Talk with a woman whom you know to have "wisdom." Ask her to share her experience of God with you.

As my response to the gospel of Jesus, this week I commit to _____

_____ .

Lifting Our Hearts

Pray alternately the Magnificat (Luke 1:46-55)

Side 1
My soul magnifies the Lord,
    and my spirit rejoices in God my Savior,
for he has looked with favor
    on the lowliness of his servant.

Side 2
Surely, from now on all generations will call me blessed;
for the Mighty One has done great things for me,
    and holy is his name.

Side 1
His mercy is for those who fear him
    from generation to generation.

Side 2
He has shown strength with his arm;
    he has scattered the proud
    in the thoughts of their hearts.

Side 1
He has brought down the powerful from their thrones,
    and lifted up the lowly;
he has filled the hungry with good things,
    and sent the rich away empty.

Side 2
He has helped his servant Israel,
    in remembrance of his mercy,
according to the promise he made to our ancestors,
    to Abraham and to his descendants forever.

Looking Ahead

- Prepare for your next session by prayerfully reading and studying **Session 12, We Believe in Life Everlasting** and paragraphs 988-1065 of the *Catechism*.

- Remember to use RENEWING FAMILY FAITH (see pages 76-77) and its helpful suggestions on how to extend the fruits of your sharing beyond your group, especially to your families.

Session 12

We Believe in Life Everlasting

✝✝✝

Suggested environment

Bible, candle, and, if possible, the *Catechism of the Catholic Church*
Begin with a quiet, reflective atmosphere.

Lifting Our Hearts

Song

"I Am the Bread of Life," Suzanne Toolan, R.S.M. (GIA)

Pray together

Father, sometimes it is difficult for us to believe in you
     and how wonderfully you have created us.
Yet we hunger to know you and to understand
     that you offer us life everlasting.
What we do not see, nor hear, nor feel,
     we do believe.
Help our unbelief.
We ask this through Christ our Lord. Amen.

Sharing Our Good News

Share how you did with your **Living the Good News** *from the previous session.*

Exploring the *Catechism*

How many times has the thought crossed our minds: "Is this all there is?" Because as a culture we are very scientific and technological at times, we sometimes do not trust what we cannot see or "prove." Yet, we proclaim in our profession of faith that we believe in God's creative, saving, and sanctifying action that culminates in the proclamation of a belief in the resurrection of our bodies and life everlasting **(988).**

Just as Jesus died and is risen from the dead and so lives forever, we, too, will live forever with the risen Jesus and we, too, will be raised up on the last day **(989)**.

God revealed the resurrection of the dead to ... people progressively (992). The Pharisees and many of those who lived at Jesus' time **hoped for the resurrection. Jesus teaches it firmly (993).** Jesus goes one step further and links faith in the resurrection with himself: "I am the resurrection and the life" (John 11:25). To believe in Jesus is to believe in life everlasting. To believe in Jesus is to believe that we will be raised up with him on the last day **(994).** Listen to Jesus' promise.

Scripture: Pondering the Word   John 6:39-40

Sharing Question

- How has my belief in the Resurrection been a comfort at the death of a loved one? How might I respond to someone who asks the question: "Is this all there is?"

Exploring the *Catechism* (continued)

From the time of the early Church, certain questions were raised: Who will rise? How do the dead rise? The Scriptures tell us that [a]ll **the dead will rise, "those who have done good, to the resurrection of life, and those who have done evil, to the resurrection of judgment"** (John 5:29, cf. Daniel 12:2) **(998). This "how" exceeds our imagination and understanding; it is accessible only to faith (1000).** But we know that each person receives **a particular judgment** at the moment of death **(1022).**

When the Father sent Jesus, we came to know that the reign of God was present to us, in the here and now. We are each united with Christ at Baptism, and thus we already participate in the life of the risen Christ. Nourished with his body, we already belong to the Body of Christ. Yet we believe there is more to come. We believe in the "already" and the "not yet." We believe that we are united to Christ, will rise with Christ on the last day, and "will appear with him in glory in his heavenly kingdom" (Colossians 3:4) **(1003).**

This perfect life with the Most Holy Trinity—this communion of life and love with the Trinity, with the Virgin Mary, the angels and all the blessed—is called "heaven."

Heaven is the ultimate end and fulfillment of the deepest human longings, the state of supreme, definitive happiness (1024).

By his death and Resurrection, Jesus Christ has "opened" heaven to us. The life of the blessed consists in the full and perfect possession of the fruits of the redemption accomplished by Christ. He makes partners in his heavenly glorification those who have believed in him and remained faithful to his will. Heaven is the blessed community of all who are perfectly incorporated into Christ (1026).

But [t]o rise with Christ, we must die with Christ (1005). Why are we often afraid of our own death? Death is not easy, because in many ways it is unknown. We try to flee from it and go to any extent to prevent it from happening until it touches our lives through the death of a loved one or through an illness or accident. Jesus promises that those who enter into death with him will enter new life. Death is a natural process, and we are encouraged to prepare ourselves for the time of our own death (1014). How important it is for us to embrace death with faith and hope!

St. John of the Cross said so knowingly: "At the evening of life, we shall be judged on our love" (1022). It is a marvelous reflection to think that at the time of our death we will be asked: "How well did you love?" Since God is love, heaven is living in that complete love. To be devoid of love is to be excluded from God. This state of definitive self-exclusion from communion with God and the blessed is called "hell" (1033).

The teaching of the Church affirms the existence of hell and its eternity. Immediately after death the souls of those who die in a state of mortal sin descend into hell, where they suffer the punishments of hell, "eternal fire." The chief punishment of hell is eternal separation from God, in whom alone man can possess the life and happiness for which he was created and for which he longs (1035).

Many persons are not devoid of love, but their love is still hindered by sins of selfishness, jealousy, avarice, lust, etc. Such persons are not able to join in the selfless love of the saints: They are not ready to give or receive the utterly unselfish love of the Divine Persons. They are not yet ready to share completely in the life of God.

Thus, the Church teaches that for those who still need to achieve such holiness after death there is a final purification—purgatory—that is entirely different from that of hell. **All who die in God's grace and friendship, but still imperfectly purified, are indeed assured of their eternal salvation; but after death they undergo purification, so as to achieve the holiness necessary to enter the joy of heaven (1030).**

In the beautiful mystery of the communion of saints, those still being purified from their sins in purgatory are linked together in a bond of love with the faithful on earth and those who have already reached heaven. **In this wonderful exchange, the holiness of one profits others … (1475).** By God's grace, our prayers and words of charity can still affect the souls of persons who have gone before us, just as the loving care of those in heaven continues to be a blessing to us who still struggle in this world.

We began these sessions with a reflection on our desire for God. Each of us has within us an innate desire for God, a desire to go home. When a child is born into this world, the child experiences the vastness and at times the "coldness" of a world so different from the mother's womb. So, too, when it is our time to die and enter into a new world, we may experience a resistance to newness, yet there is the wonder of so much more than we could ask for or imagine. There have been many wonderful stories of people who have had "near death" experiences, who have shared about the light they saw and how they were not afraid, but rather welcomed the warmth and the attractiveness of the light. The positive nature of these experiences is optimistic and hopeful. However, such experiences should be viewed in terms of Christian tradition. It may be only after we have entered into eternal life that we will fully realize that we were only pilgrims on this earth.

While it may be difficult for us to even imagine, we are promised that at the end of time, God's reign **will come in its fullness (1042).** In the Book of Revelation (chapter 21), we are promised that in this new universe, God will dwell fully among us. The direct experience of God will wipe away every tear from our eyes and death shall be no more **(1044).** For us as human beings there will be the final realization of the unity of the human race that the Lord created **(1043).** For our universe, there will be a full transformation and fulfillment. We will no longer see ourselves as separate, but at one with God's universe. We will dwell in harmony in this new heaven and new earth in which righteousness dwells, in which our happiness will fill and surpass all the desire of peace arising out of our hearts **(1048).**

Sharing Our Faith

- How would I respond if at the "evening of my life" I am asked, "How did you love?"
- How often do I make the mistake of thinking that *my own* goodness will save me, rather than the goodness of God?
- How do I feel about dying? What are my fears? What are my hopes? How might I prepare for death?

Living the Good News

Determine a specific action (individual or group) that flows from your sharing. This should be your primary consideration.

When choosing an individual action, determine what you will do and share it with the group. When choosing a group action, determine who will take responsibility for different aspects of the action.

The following are secondary suggestions:

- Continue to meet as a small community using one of the three other books in this *Why Catholic? Journey through the Catechism Series:*
  The Celebration of the Christian Mystery: Sacraments
  Life in Christ: Walking with God
  Christian Prayer: Deepening My Experience of God.
- Put some ideas together for your own funeral liturgy. Give them to someone close to you so they can be used at your funeral.
- Journal your feelings about death or compose a letter to God revealing your feelings about death.

- If possible, talk with someone who may be near death. Offer your assistance to someone who has lost a loved one.
- Celebrate in a special way with your group through a prayer or social event.

As my response to the gospel of Jesus, this week I commit to _____

_____ .

Lifting Our Hearts

Song "I Am the Resurrection," Balhoff, Ducote and Daigle, OCP.

Sing or play the song. Listen carefully to the words.

Then in your own words, express your belief.

(For example: I do believe, O God, that you have prepared a place for me for all eternity.)

Conclude by praying together the Apostles' Creed on pages 17-18.

Looking Ahead

- Remember to use RENEWING FAMILY FAITH (see pages 76-77) and its helpful suggestions on how to extend the fruits of your sharing beyond your group, especially to your families.
- To continue faith sharing between Seasons of *Why Catholic?* you may want to use the appropriate cycle of PRAYERTIME: *Faith-Sharing Reflections on the Sunday Gospels*, Cycle A, B, or C. (For information, see page 78.)
- Alternatively, you may find that many of theme based faith-sharing resources in the **IMPACT** Series suits the interests of your group. (See page 78 for details.)

Music Resources

GIA

For CDs, printed music, downloadable mp3 files and permission to reprint words and/or music, contact:
GIA Publications, Inc.
7404 South Mason Avenue
Chicago, IL 60638
Phone   800-442-1358 or 708-496-3800
Fax   708-496-3828
Website   www.giamusic.com
E-mail   custserv@giamusic.com

OCP

For CDs, printed music, downloadable mp3 files (via iTunes) contact:
Oregon Catholic Press Publications
5536 NE Hassalo
Portland, OR 97213
Phone   800-LITURGY (548-8749)
Fax   800-4-OCP-FAX (462-7329)
Website   www.ocp.org
E-mail   liturgy@ocp.org

For permission to reprint words and/or music, contact:
www.licensingonline.org

RENEW

For cassettes of the RENEW the Face of the Earth *albums, contact:*
RENEW International
1232 George Street
Plainfield, NJ 07062-1717
To order   888-433-3221
Fax   908-769-5660
Website   www.renewintl.org

White Dove

For CDs and song books of the RENEW the Face of the Earth *albums, contact:*
White Dove Productions, Inc.
Phone   520-219-3824
Website   www.whitedoveproductions.com
E-mail   info@whitedoveproductions.com

Further Reading

Pope John Paul II. Post-Synodal Apostolic Exhortation, *The Lay Members of Christ's Faithful People (Christifideles Laici)*.
Available online at:
www.vatican.va/holy_father/john_paul_ii/apost_exhortations/documents/hf_jp-ii_exh_30121988_christifideles-laici_en.html
Printed edition is available from: Boston, MA: Pauline Books & Media, 1988.

Committee on the Laity, United States Conference of Catholic Bishops. *Lay Ecclesial Ministry: The State of the Questions*. Washington, DC, United States Conference of Catholic Bishops, 1999.

United States Conference of Catholic Bishops. *Mary in the Church: A Selection of Teaching Documents*. Washington, DC, United States Conference of Catholic Bishops, 2003.

RENEW International. *PRAYERTIME: Faith-Sharing Reflections on the Sunday Gospels*, Cycle A (2001), B (2002), C (2000, 2006). Plainfield, NJ: RENEW International.

Why Catholic? Resources from RENEW

RENEWING FAMILY FAITH:

We Believe, We Celebrate, We Live, We Pray

RENEWING FAMILY FAITH is a resource designed to extend the experience of the *Why Catholic?* process so that the faith sharing it promotes can become an integral part of whole family catechesis.

For every Session offered by the *Why Catholic?* faith-sharing books there is a corresponding practical, informative two-page bulletin in full color: a total of 48 in all (12 for each of the four *Why Catholic?* faith-sharing books).

These Bulletins have been produced to facilitate sharing within the family on exactly the same themes the adults are exploring together in their *Why Catholic?* faith-sharing sessions.

Each issue offers:

- an interesting selection of faith reflections for parents
- a wide variety of family activities
- questions that encourage table sharing
- brief scripture passages and wisdom quotes
- an inspiring story on the life of an honored saint or a modern person who has lived an extraordinary faith life

This is a resource which can serve in a variety of creative ways: to reach and assist those whom for some reason are unable to take part in the Sunday celebration of Mass: those who are the sick or homebound.

It can also be used in sacramental preparation programs, and for homily preparation.

Here is the content for each Bulletin, designed to correspond and complement the Sessions in this *Profession of Faith* faith-sharing book:

1. **Desire for God**
   Our Story: Dorothy Day
   Parenting: Communication
   Family Activities: Searching for
      God's Presence
   Pondering the Word: Luke 12:32
   CCC: 27

2. **God's Revelation:**
   Tradition and Scripture
   Our Story: Singing Nun (Sr. Thea
      Bowman)
   Parenting: Evening Reflection
   Family Activities: Two-Minute
      Quiz
   Pondering the Word: 2 Peter 1:20-21
   CCC: 110

3. **Faith: I Believe, We Believe**
Our Story: Believing Thomas
Parenting: Faith Development
Family Activities: Faith Sharing
CCC: 162-163

4. **The Trinity**
Our Story: Karl Rahner
Parenting: Wholeness in Life
Family Activities: Family Night
Pondering the Word: John 14:26
CCC: 249

5. **The Mystery of Creation**
Our Story: St. Francis of Assisi
Parenting: Self-Renewal
Family Activities: Jesus and
  Individualism
Pondering the Word: Genesis 1:1
CCC: 314

6. **Keep Your Eyes and Ears Open**
Our Story: First American Saint
  (Elizabeth Anne Seton)
Parenting: Faces of Racism
Family Activities: Family
  Communication
Pondering the Word: John 1:1
CCC: 463

7. **Public Life of Jesus**
Our Story: Preferential Option for
  the Poor (Selection from Joseph
  Cardinal Bernardin, 1988)
Parenting: Spiritual Needs
Family Activities: The Mind of
  Jesus
Pondering the Word: Luke 4:18
CCC: 543

8. **The Paschal Mystery:
Jesus' Death and Resurrection**
Our Story: Oscar Romero –
  Prophet and Martyr
Parenting: Parents' Role in
  Cultural Change
Family Activities: Family Priorities
Pondering the Word: Mark 8:27

9. **The Holy Spirit and the Church**
Our Story: Vocation (Thomas
  Merton)
Parenting: Emotional Intelligence
Family Activities: What is Love?
Pondering the Word: 1 Cor 2:12
CCC: 738

10. **A Family with Many Parts**
Our Story: Early Disciples
  (Priscilla and Aquila)
Parenting: Active Listening
Family Activities: Children's Books
Pondering the Word: John 17:20-21
CCC: 900

11. **Mary, Mother of Christ,
Mother of the Church**
Our Story: Theotokos (Bearer of
  God)
Parenting: Two Myths about
  Conflict
Family Activities: How to Criticize
  Effectively
Pondering the Word: Luke 1:38
CCC: 967

12. **We Believe in Life Everlasting**
Our Story: Mother Teresa
Parenting: First-Hand Experience
Family Activities: Evening Prayer
Pondering the Word: John 6:40
CCC: 1024

PRAYERTIME Cycle A, B, C:
Faith-Sharing Reflections on the Sunday Gospels

A treasured resource responding to the U.S. Bishops' suggestion for adult faith formation that "every parish meeting can begin with the reading of the upcoming Sunday's Gospel, followed by a time of reflection and faith sharing."

Using the Sunday gospels as the focus, meaningful reflections, focused faith-sharing questions, related actions for consideration, and prayers on each Sunday reading are proposed as a source for nourishment, renewal, and inspiration.

PRAYERTIME is published in three editions, one for each of the three years in the liturgical cycle.

It is recommended *PRAYERTIME* be used by groups between seasons of *Why Catholic?* at parish pastoral council and parish staff meetings, at the beginning of other parish group meetings, and for personal reflection.

The IMPACT Series

The **IMPACT** Series aims to connect faith to a wide range of human concerns and personal issues. In the process, participants will not only be led to prayerful reflection and fruitful sharing but also to concrete actions that influence attitudes and behaviors.

Growth through action is a basic principle in the **IMPACT** Series. In addition to encouraging discussion and sharing, this series leads to concrete action. Many issues are somewhat difficult to face and to grasp. Experience shows that such issues are seldom addressed without a certain amount of challenge, guidance, and assistance.

The **IMPACT** Series is designed to meet this need and, in doing so, to help small Christian communities realize better their great potential for ushering in the fullness of God's reign on our earth.

Each book offers at least six faith-sharing sessions on a theme. The books in the Series are arranged in four major thematic groupings:

- Faith in Daily Life (on topics such as work, bereavement, parenting, family)
- Sacramental Pathways (including preparing children for Baptism, or for first Eucharist)
- Discipleship in Action (on topics such as racism, capital punishment, civic responsibility)
- Spiritual Awakenings (with titles such as *At Prayer with Mary*, or *Awakening the Mystic Within*)

Other Resources

Catechism of the Catholic Church
(Paperback, second edition)

> Contains the full statement of official Catholic doctrine, the essential and fundamental content of Catholic faith and morals. This second edition, published by the United States Conference of Catholic Bishops, includes revisions that were made in accordance with the official Latin text promulgated by Pope John Paul II.

Leader's Guide to Our Hearts Were Burning Within Us:
A Pastoral Plan for Adult Faith Formation in the United States
by the United States Conference of Catholic Bishops

> Part I of this two-part leader's guide edition contains rich resources to assist diocesan and parish leaders and those responsible for adult faith formation in implementing the directives of *Our Hearts Were Burning Within Us.*

> Part II contains the full U.S. Bishops' pastoral plan outlining this call to renew efforts to foster adult faith formation. The *Why Catholic?* process fosters the efforts of this plan.

All of the Resources presented on pages 76-79 of this book are available from:

> RENEW International Resources
> 1232 George Street
> Plainfield, NJ 07062-1717

Telephone (for inquiries)	908-769-5400
Toll free (for orders only)	1-888-433-3221
Fax	908-769-5660
Email	Resources@renewintl.org

and from our secure Online Bookstore:
> www.renewintl.org

Notes